FOR LOVE

OR

MONEY

From Heart to Head and Back Again

By Bert Wolfe, D.D.

The Most Important Financial Decisions You Will Ever Make

$

Financial Advice No One Dared Give You

Look Before You Leap

"The truth is, most Americans are heavily indebted, tax-paying, wage slaves."

~Bert Wolfe

I dedicate this book to my extraordinary wife. Marrying her was the best decision I have ever made.

Author's Notes

This is meant to be a no-nonsense guide to the proposition of marriage.

This book could be called Look Before You Leap: A Marriage Contemplation Guide.

This book was written from a heterosexual man's perspective. Please don't be surprised.

This book has unusual formatting. It is intentional.

This book features running lists of questions, thought prompts, and self-reflective inquiries.

This book is repetitious and redundant, and repetitive. The repetition is deliberate.

To become competent and expert at anything, we must *repeatedly practice, drill, and rehearse.*

Repetition works, repetition works, repetition works.

Reread this.

Note: The U. S. Department of Repetition and Redundancy Department approves these notes.

This book is less a treatise and more a compilation of ideas; more a reference book than a textbook;

meant to trigger ideas and move your thinking forward rapidly.

Skip the lists if you like. Read the book out of order if you like.

The book is purposely vague and repetitious; it is my job to trigger your thinking and your job to draw conclusions and make informed decisions.

I have no answers;

I have drawn few conclusions.

When I started this book, my working title was "Look Before You Leap."

I want you to think before you make the big life decisions.

I want you to have an extra-ordinary life.

Introduction

Poverty sucks.

I was so broke in my twenties that I lived in East Oakland.

East Oakland is rough, and no one lives there unless they have little choice. It's one of those places from which you need to escape.

During that dues-paying period, I had a couple of life-changing realizations.

I was trying to borrow money to buy a used pick-up truck. Several banks turned me down, and I eventually scored a usury loan from a notorious finance company.

One of the bankers who turned me down seemed wise, so I asked him for advice on getting my financial life together. His advice consisted mainly of trite platitudes, but *conventional wisdom* was one phrase he used repetitively. He suggested that a person do this, that, and the other thing. It was probably good enough advice if I wanted an ordinary life with a wife, a dog, a cat, and 2.5 kids with a white picket fence in the suburbs.

I wanted to be more than another exhausted, tax-paying, wage slave for the rest of my life.

I spent weeks contemplating all of this when it hit me that if I followed and applied *conventional wisdom*, I would end up with a conventional life. I didn't want a conventional life! I didn't exactly want an *unconventional* life, but I didn't want an *ordinary* one.

"The opposite of courage in our society is not cowardice...
it is conformity."
~ Earl Nightingale

What I wanted was an extra-ordinary life. An *extraordinary* life!

So, I realized I would need to break with conventional wisdom to achieve an extraordinary life.

I have spent my life discovering *unconventional* ways to build an unbelievable life - a life that has flourished beyond my dreams.

A second realization came while driving that old truck up out of Berkeley on Ashby Avenue one night. In front of me, a beat-up old Volvo was chugging and smoking up the hill in my misaligned headlights. A worse car than mine! Its rear bumper was missing a bolt, so it bobbed up and down, sparking off the pavement whenever the Volvo hit a good bump. I was mesmerized by this sad spectacle when I noticed a faded sticker peeling off the loose end of the bumper.

The bumper sticker said:

POVERTY SUCKS

Let's agree: POVERTY SUCKS.

That should probably be the title of this book. POVERTY SUCKS.

But what also sucks is that making *pretty good money* isn't enough. Being reasonably well-paid and still feeling broke and deeply in debt also sucks. The truth is most Americans are heavily indebted, tax-paying, wage slaves.

My two life-changing realizations:

I must have an extraordinary life.

Poverty Sucks.

Don't be fooled by how obvious and simplistic this may sound. Simple realizations are the most powerful. There is no confusion with simple concepts; only ignorance and lack of planning prevent you from creating an extraordinary life.

You have personal control over your ignorance and lack of planning. You can educate yourself and plan, in detail, for your success. This book informs and helps you make plans and establish policies that will support you in achieving the life of your dreams.

Basics to creating an extraordinary life:

Target your learning; acquire relevant wisdom.

Develop and consistently apply your life plan.

To have an extraordinary life and to avoid poverty, we need a detailed plan that includes what we *will do* and especially what *we won't do* - and when.

This book will open your eyes to the unexamined *conventional wisdom* that may sabotage your life. This book will also help you develop *plans* and *personal policies* to lead you to the extraordinary life of your dreams.

> *"If you fail to plan, you are planning to fail!"*
> *~ Benjamin Franklin*

The concept of this book is to pose questions and ideas designed to provoke higher levels of *thoughtful decision-making*. I want to encourage you and me to be more awake and aware. And more thoughtful about the decisions we make as we stumble through life.

Will your choices and decisions support the values and qualities you want to be consistently present?

Qualities of your life:

- Love
- Romance
- Enjoyment

- Fun
- Pleasure
- Adventure
- Accomplishment
- Professional success
- Personal Recognition
- Satisfaction
- Life-long learning
- Fulfilling parenting
- Rewarding family life
- Travel
- Good health
- Fitness
- Low stress
- Spiritual insight
- Financial freedom

Life is rigorous, and most of us don't get much useful help along the way. We need to help our own selves, and we need to take care of the outcomes of our own lives.

Let's be honest; nobody gets everything right. We all foul up sometimes, but what if you could minimize or avoid some of the most damaging pitfalls that conventional wisdom might steer you toward?

This book is about minimizing pitfalls and helping people identify and avoid pitfalls.

Most people live their lives by *default*. Most people don't make calculated, conscious decisions. Most people do *what they are supposed to* or *what everybody else does*. Or, they wait until forced by *circumstances* to do some last-minute fix on some clumsy goof-up. Most people are *winging it* through life.

For example, if you fail to file a tax return, the IRS will find you and force some ill-timed, non-optimum *solution* on you. Even if you file on time but have no knowledge about or plan for controlling your taxes, the IRS will have its way with you.

For example, if you fail to use birth control without specific plans for a baby, you will eventually have an ill-timed child for whom you will have an 18-year financial responsibility.

For example, if you are not using condoms while dating, you will likely contract a nasty, perhaps incurable, disease.

For example, if you are a man who depends on a woman to handle birth control, you will likely find yourself on the hook for a child. Why would you leave something that important to someone else?

Living by default means operating indiscriminately with no plans or policies, winging it, and getting *default* results.

I suppose, occasionally, *shit happens.* But you won't hear a successful person use the excuse *shit happens.* Life sometimes dumps random trouble on us, but how we handle it, based on pre-thought-out policies and careful planning, will control the outcome of even the worst *acts of God.* Much of the bad stuff that happens to people is predictable and avoidable with better knowledge and forethought.

I hear the excuse, "Well, people have to learn somehow." Or "Well, that's how we learn." It may be true to some degree, but I mostly disagree. We *can* learn from others, we *can* learn from the mistakes of others, and **we can learn from the success patterns of others.** We don't need to stumble through life.

We don't have to discover everything for ourselves. After all, we go to school – to learn what others before us have learned the hard way.

I once overheard a mother lamenting the foolish behavior of her adolescent son: "Honest to God, I don't know if that boy has a brain in his head. **For love or money,** he won't listen to a thing I say. He refuses to plan or even *think* most of the time. He just doesn't have **good sense.**"

This mother's diatribe struck me hard.

Sometimes, we refuse to take good advice. Sometimes, we won't listen. We don't need to *learn everything the hard way.* If we had the humility and good sense to learn from other's mistakes and successes, we could go further and grow faster in our own lives.

Another failure pattern is just doing what feels good in the moment or just *living by the heart* --letting life take you wherever it will. *Don't worry, be happy.* Oh, sure; we see how poorly that works for people all around us.

A narrative goes something like this: "I just let my life drift along *catch as catch can,* and things have worked out okay. I am still alive. I've had some fun."

Okay, so be it. But, upon more in-depth interviews, these people consistently report a lifetime of serious financial trouble and ruined relationships. These are not the people who achieve deep satisfaction from an extraordinary life.

Is this book all about money? No, maybe yes. The point is that whatever your higher purposes are, you can serve them better when you are not financially stressed.

Everyone has regrets, but why build a life of them? Keep your attention off regrets and focus on the present and the future you are creating. When you are on your *deathbed,* you will want to feel that you built something meaningful and helped some people and want to feel like you *achieved* in some significant way.

This book will help you build a heartfelt, analytical plan for creating an *extraordinary,* fun, and fulfilling life.

Study this book and then give it to someone you care about.

"The spirit of a man is constructed out of his choices."

~ Irvin D. Yalom

"All you need is the plan, the road map, and the courage to press on to your destination."

~Earl Nightingale

"When you were born, you crie d, and the world rejoiced. Live your life in such a manner that when you die, the world cries, and you rejoice."

~Chief Seattle

Contents

Chapter 1 Dating

"Most people who have made it through dating never want to do it again."

~Bert Wolfe

The purpose of dating is to hunt for and find a lifelong mate. Dating to get laid can confuse matters. Especially with the advent of internet dating, the essential purpose of finding a mate might get obscured when participating in the so-called *hookup* culture. Putting frivolous fun aside, dating needs to be a focused endeavor. Time is short, especially for women who would like to bear children. The childbearing pressure is less for men, but the longer a man waits, the longer it will take to execute his life plan. It may be tactically adventitious to find a suitable mate as soon as possible and start building a lifetime marriage and family.

Time is of the Essence
Lie: "There is plenty of time to find a spouse."
Wrong! Lie!

Truth: Women who want children are especially under the pressure of time.

Suggested age/time frames:

- Dating: 16-25 years of age; learning who not to marry and procreate with - finding a suitable mate.

- Marriage: 25-30 years of age; finding a sane "grown-up" spouse. Churn spouses if necessary to acquire a lifetime spouse.

- Procreation: 25-35 years of age; make babies with a sensible plan.

- Lasting marriage; 30-100 years of age; build a stable, productive family that endures the tests of time—continuous hard work; pleasantly tedious; total loyalty required; intermittently fun.

Most people date too long. They fail to date with the intention of being married sooner rather than later. Presuming you want children, you must have established a stable, permanent spouse, house, and career by age forty. Let's say you finish college by age 26 and must be permanently set up by age 40. For women, safe procreation needs to be completed before age 35. That is less than 15 years to find a permanent house, spouse, and career, which is a lot to accomplish. You must be focused and committed to a specific detailed plan. Obstructions, delays, and counter intentions must not be tolerated. Distractions and barriers must be blasted out of the way.

Hopefully, you get some fun and enjoyment while dating, but there is little time to waste. Hard work is unavoidable.

Potential Sources of Limitations, Barriers, and Counter Intentions:

- Parents
- Spouses
- Teachers
- Bosses
- Colleagues
- Bankers
- Government
- Friends
- Enemies
- Frenemies
- Religion
- Ideology
- Culture
- Ethnic traditions
- Socio-economics
- Education
- Social class

Be a Train and Build a Railroad

Railroads have the highest priority in all transportation infrastructures. Automotive roads are built to stop, look, and listen for a train, or else the highway goes over or under the railroad. Trains don't stop for automobiles. Railroads have the most potent eminent domain. Railroads "stay on track" while automobile roads wander around everywhere. Railroads are set; they deliver trains to their destinations reliably and predictably.

Design your life path like a metaphorical railroad. Set your tracks and demand primacy as you pursue your life's ambitions.

In the locomotive industry, a cow catcher is a shallow, V-shaped wedge mounted to the front of a train engine designed to deflect obstacles from the track at a reasonably high speed without disrupting the smooth progress of the train.

Set your tracks and drive a powerful engine with a cow catcher on the front that clears all obstacles.

Let nothing stop you from finding your mate as soon as possible.

The Hunt

How to prospect for a mate:

- Professional matchmaking
- Internet dating sites
- Set-ups by mutual friends
- Family set-ups
- School
- Church
- Common-interest activity clubs
- Volunteer work
- Ask your friends and family to set you up with a quality person. Friends and family know you the best.

The Husband Store Joke

A store that sells husbands has opened in New York City. When women go to choose a husband, they must abide by the following instructions:

"You may visit this store only once. There are six floors, and the attributes of the men increase as the shopper ascends the flights. On each floor, you may choose a man or choose to go up to the next floor, but you cannot go back down except to exit the building!"

So, a woman goes to The Husband Store to procure a husband.

On the first floor, the sign on the door reads:

Floor 1 – These men have jobs and love kids.

She decides to go up to the second floor. The second-floor sign reads:

Floor 2 – These men have jobs, love kids, and love God.

She chooses to move up. The third-floor sign reads:

Floor 3 – These men have jobs, love kids, love God, and are handsome.

"Wow," she exclaims but feels compelled to keep going. She goes to the fourth floor, and the sign reads:

Floor 4 – These men have jobs, love kids, love God, are handsome, and help with the housework.

"Oh, my!" she exclaims. "I can hardly believe it!" Still, she goes to the fifth floor, where the sign reads:

Floor 5 – These men have jobs, love kids, love God, are handsome, help with the housework, and have a strong romantic streak.

Intuitively, she knows this is the correct floor. Nevertheless, she goes on to the sixth floor, and the sign reads:

Floor 6 – You are visitor 4,363,012. No men exist on this floor because this floor exists solely to prove that women are impossible to please. Thank you for shopping at the Husband Store. Please exit the building.

To avoid accusations of gender bias, the owner of The Husband Store opened a store across the street called The Wife Store.

The 1st floor has wives who love sex.

The 2nd floor has wives who love sex and have money.

The 3rd through 6th floors have never been visited.

Where not to prospect for a mate:

- Bars and nightclubs
- Your place of work
- Married people
- Hook-up websites

"Before you marry someone, sit in traffic with them for at least two hours."

~Unknown

"Divorce is a financial disaster from which you can never fully recover."

~Bert Wolfe

Divorces are Catastrophic Setbacks

If you are not solidly sure your prospective spouse is committing to a lifetime marriage, don't marry that person.

There are endless resources for marital help. Marriage requires constant work. After choosing your person, you keep choosing them no matter what. Tough it out through the challenging periods, no matter how tough and long.

It is unrealistic to hold a standard of some fantasy perfect marriage. Create a good enough marriage and get on with building, protecting, and enjoying it.

Frankly, most people are deeply flawed, imperfect human beings. Don't dwell on your mate's faults and mistakes. If your spouse consistently carries their weight, overlook their mistakes and foibles. If they embarrass you occasionally or mess up, disregard it and move forward.

For instance, if they embarrass you somehow, tell them about it and drop it.

For instance, if they dent the car, say nothing and get it repaired immediately.

Don't get married if you don't think you can grace your mate.

If your mate does something catastrophically wrong and you cannot live with it, break up quickly and rebuild your life without delay.

Basis of Choice

Attraction

What attracts women:

- Fat wallet
- Competence
- Confidence
- Provider
- Protector

- Prestige
- Power
- Influence

The Sixes:

- Six figures
- Six pack
- Six feet
- Six inches

What attracts men:

- Fit
- Friendly
- Feminine
- Long hair
- Demure
- Agreeable
- Respectful
- Regular sex
- Domestic tranquility
- Loyalty

"Women practice hypergamy.

They seek men of higher socioeconomic status."

~Bert Wolfe

Women look *up* for a superior marriage partner:

- Money up
- Car up
- Height up
- Body count up
- Mental strength up
- Competence up
- Age up
- Masculinity up
- Physical strength up
- Leadership up
- Power, status, and influence up

Women Avoid:

- Poor wallet
- Poor grooming
- Low self-confidence
- Laziness

- Crappy car
- Wimps
- Simps
- Pussies
- Betas
- Immaturity
- Boring
- Low self-esteem
- Nice guys

"Men are cost/benefit calculators."

~**Kevin Samuels**

Men look *down* for a subordinate marriage partner:

- Car down
- Money down
- Height down
- Weight down
- Body count down
- Age down
- Masculinity down
- Body fat down
- Bossiness down

Men Avoid *High-Maintenance* Women:

- Expensive tastes
- Emotionally needy
- Psychologically demanding
- Time vampires
- DIY husband improvers
- Amateur nutritionists
- Substitute mothers
- Dissatisfaction machines
- Critics
- Complainers
- Argue addicts
- Disagreeableness
- Contrarians

Practicalities of Relative Personal Value

What women want from a marriage partner:

- Stability (long-term commitment)
- Financial security
- Protection
- Confidence
- Leadership
- Good presentation
- Strong and fit
- Stoic behavior

- Chivalry

- Romance

- Attention

- Good listening

- Admiration

What men want from a marriage partner:

- Loyalty

- Reliable sex

- Respect

- Sustained physical attraction (fitness)

- Femininity (softness)

- Peace (quiet domestic tranquility)

- Physical fitness

- Long hair

- Cooperation

- Agreeableness

- She takes his side

- Diminutive behavior

- Psychological support

- Care and feeding

"An ideal marriage would be a rich, blind husband and a mute, agreeable wife."

~Bert Wolfe

What About Love?

I don't list love as a value because it is an undefinable, amorphous concept. No two people agree on what love is.

Men want respect. Women want admiration. If a couple can establish a relationship based on respect and admiration, then something approximating love will develop and grow.

Some couples are strongly attracted to one another, which might be some form of love.

Since love is so difficult to define, I look for other qualities of attraction that are easier to identify.

If a person strategically chooses a partner based on specific criteria rather than going simply with *feelings*, I believe the outcome is more likely to be viable.

It is observable that women who run a lot of masculine energy are more frustrated and unhappy. The analog is that men who run a lot of feminine energy are more frustrated and unhappy.

Masculine men and feminine women appear to be more satisfied both individually and together.

Modern feminists and emasculated men will tend to be nervous, lonely, and frustrated.

Men and Women have Different Powers:

- Women control access to sex and procreation.
- Men control access to relationships and marriage.

Considerations of Past and Future

Dating

Men:

When dating, a man is interested in the woman's *past* to determine her probable predilections, choices, and staying power. A high body count and/or negative past relationships are not good signs. The man does not want a bitter woman who habitually compares him to her past lovers. Women with lower body counts tend to bond more readily.

Men are looking for a woman with a wholesome and perhaps naïve past.

He will be looking for a devoted and agreeable woman. Men are attracted to sexual purity. Sexual purity could be described as not having been promiscuous and having a low body count.

Men need devotion, peace, and loyalty.

Women:

A woman will be considering the man's *future*. Will he be able to fulfill her needs? She expects him to improve and prosper. She is concerned with future protection and provisioning. Will he continue to love her?

Women need admiration, appreciation, and security.

Bottom Line:

Men want loyalty and respect.

Women want security, admiration, and romance.

They both need appreciation from each other.

Why men are reluctant to marry:

- Women control access to sex.
- One out of four marriages is sexless.

- Sixty percent of marriages end in divorce.
- Women control procreation (wanted babies may not occur) (but unwanted babies can occur.)
- Women initiate eighty percent of divorces (90% when college-educated.)
- $20K in legal fees for divorce.
- The woman will get over half of the man's net worth.
- The woman will keep the house, furniture, kids, pets, and the best car.
- The man and his toys get evicted, and he becomes temporarily but essentially homeless.
- The man's home life can be reduced to a college-level lifestyle.
- The woman will control access to the children.
- Men are significantly more damaged emotionally by divorce.

The cost of legal fees, property division, and child support can be substantial. Divorcing couples may also experience a loss of income, as both partners will be distracted and need to take time off work to deal with the divorce process.

Divorce could cost:

- $40K combined legal fees
- $500K half of the stuff
- $500K half the house
- $700K alimony (7 years)
- $550K child support (two children,15 years)
- $20K dating
- $20K career advancement stall and productivity drop
- $5K counseling

Total: $2,335,000

Don't believe it? Cut this number in half, or do your own calculations. Anyway you figure it, divorce is a financial catastrophe.

Survey Says:

- Sex is excellent for men while dating.
- Sex will diminish noticeably after engagement.
- Sex will dramatically decrease after the wedding.
- Chances are high that there will be no sex on the wedding night.
- 25% of marriages are sexless.

Remember, women control access to sex.

Open Questions:

Why would a man want to get married?

- Because she demands it.

Why do most men get married anyway?

- Because "everybody" does it.

For over twenty years, I have challenged men with a hundred-dollar reward if they can give me one good reason for a man to get married. No one has gotten the hundred dollars off of me.

I have gotten three ponderable answers so far:

Marry a rich girl: Okay, if that is why you are getting married, you are no better than a female gold-digger. That psychology is fantastically unmasculine and unacceptable.

Because she is pregnant: I will not even dignify that extorsion. What is she doing pregnant out of wedlock? And if that is how she operates, why do you even think it is your child?

Because she won't stay with me unless we get married: ("Marry me, or I will leave you for someone who will.") That may be the most common reason men get married, but it is not wholesome. It is extortion and terrorism. Plus, what makes you think she will stay after you are married?

For most couples, marriage is emasculating.

It seems that most people get married out of social tradition; she expects it, and everybody does it.

"If you've met your soulmate by age 22, great. But the truth is, most people don't."

~Meghan Daum

Syndicated Columnist

"Good husbands are harder to find than good jobs."

~Yvonne Brill

Rocket Scientist

Spouse candidate and selection charts:

For the Man, the woman must be:

Entrepreneur/Owner	Professional/Management	Trades/Early Career
Beautiful	Cute	Sexy
Intelligent	Smart	Clever
Graduate degree	College degree	High school or GED
Professional	Career	Good job
Self-employed	Management	Employment
Rotary	Kiwanis	Lions
Private Club	Country Club	Eagles Club
Elegant	Stylish	Alluring
Domestic car	European car	Japanese car

For the Woman, the Man Must Be:

Entrepreneur/Owner	Professional/Management	Trades/Early Career
Presentable	Handsome	Cute
Intelligent	Smart	Clever
Dry humor	Entertaining	Funny
Profession	Job Title	Trade
Self-employed	Management	Employment
Rotary	Kiwanis	Lions
Dressed to occasion	Current styles	Laborer Chic
Private Club	Country Club	Eagles Club
Good Hygiene	Good grooming	Rough
Older domestic sedan or truck	European sports car	Rice burner w/modified exhaust and trunk wing

Before prospecting for a functional mate, you must clarify and focus your search criteria.

"If you can't name it, you can't claim it."

~Unknown

Hunt, Capture, Retain

Search, Find, Keep

Most people have an ill-formed, half-baked version of knowing what they want in a mate, but almost worse; they rarely consider what their prospective mate may want from *them*. We must consider what our future mate wants and expect from us and the relationship. What do you have to offer? Why would they choose you? – specifically – over all others?

Since you will probably still get married:

- Make a thoughtful choice of spouse.
- Work to fulfill each other's needs.
- Be loyal.
- Be consistent.
- Have a plan and follow it.
- Make agreements and keep them.
- Study this book together.

Make a Sensible Choice

One can be attracted to and *fall in love* with any number of people. So, select wisely. When you analytically find someone who fits the bill *on paper*, you will naturally admire and respect them. Admiration and respect are the basis of enduring love. Find someone you can admire and respect, then grow in love with them. That's a better formula for success than randomly *falling in love* – or, more like, *falling in lust*.

Beware of choosing a mate by pheromones alone. Don't fall for *falling in love*; it's the hormones and pheromones talking.

We try to find the most suitable spouse within the time allotted. When we find ourselves single, we shop (date) for a new mate. We yearn for a companion and are eager to fill the void soon. Sooner is always good, but a right choice is more critical. Since you will be shopping, take enough time and be a wise shopper.

Forget about finding your *one and only*. There is no such thing.

You are not looking for *the* right partner; you are looking for *a* right partner.

Look for:

- Mr. Right Enough
- Mr. More Than Sufficient
- Mr. Good Enough
- Mr. Appropriate
- Mr. Strategic
- Mr. More Than Adequate
- Mr. Makes Sense
- Mr. Suitable
- Mr. Appropriate
- Mr. Empowering
- Mr. Lifetime

"But I don't want to settle for someone who is only just good enough!" Yes, you do.

"I want someone *amazing*." Probably not.

"I want someone who *completes* me." Why? Are you incomplete or deficient in some way?

Deeply consider what you want marriage to be about. Seriously, why are you getting married in the first place, and why that person?

"You may not be her first, her last, or her only. She loved before; she may love again. But if she loves you now, what else matters? She's not perfect—you aren't either, and the two of you may never be perfect together, but if she can make you laugh, cause you to think twice, and admit to being human and making mistakes, hold onto her and give her the most you can. She may not be thinking about you every second of the day, but she will give you a part of her that she knows you can break—her heart. So don't hurt her, don't change her, don't analyze, and don't expect more than she can give. Smile when she makes you happy, let her know when she makes you mad, and miss her when she's not there."

~Bob Marley

Alternatives to Marriage

Ask yourself:

- Are there viable legal alternatives to marriage? (Yes)
- Marriage is a contract. Do you need a binding legal agreement to keep you together? (Maybe)

You want someone who empowers or enhances you, can stand independently the way you do, and is synergistic with you.

$1 + 1 = 3$

"What I need is someone who can make me do what I can."

~Ralph Waldo Emerson

"Sex is the great leveler; taste is the great divider."

~Pauline Dail, For Keeps

"You can have sex with and bond with any number of people, but choosing your most essential life partner requires a decidedly judicious approach."

~Bert Wolfe

Know Before You Go

"Warning – never marry (or get engaged to) a stranger.

~H. Norman Wright

Before You Say I Do

"Who you choose to marry is the most important financial decision you will ever make."

~Bert Wolfe

Do you actually know this person?

Long ago, I was trained and licensed as a notary public. A Notary Public is an official witness to the signing of legal documents. They *serve as an impartial witness to deter fraud.* A Notary Public must verify a signer's identity by personal knowledge. Personal knowledge means the notary has known the signer for an extended period and is confident the signer has the identity claimed. *Personally known* means having an acquaintance derived from association with the individual, establishing the individual's identity with reasonable certainty.

So, how well do you know your prospective mate? Marry someone strange if you want, but don't marry a stranger.

I dated Sue for a couple of years. I grew very fond of her. At one point, I provisionally suggested marriage and got an amused negative response. It was a setback, but I was pretty into her. I was becoming frustrated with the progress of our relationship. She kept me in mystery and treated me like a boy toy. We lived about ninety miles apart. She insisted that I come to her. I could never get her to visit my cool place in Santa Cruz. I basically ignored this. She wasn't sinister or anything, just noncommittal. I'm the commitment type of guy.

One day, she told me I needed to take her out for her birthday. I realized I didn't even know her birthday! Is that important information? Probably.

Anyway, I asked what day her birthday was; she said Saturday. I laughed and told her Saturday was my birthday. She thought I was pulling a gag. I believed she was pulling a gag. I couldn't figure out how she knew my birthday, but *obviously,* she was getting us out to celebrate my birthday.

Out on the sidewalk, she tossed me the keys to her sportscar and said, "Here, it's my birthday, you drive." As we walked to the back of her car, I noticed for the first time her license plate frame read, "Happiness is Being Single." Uh oh, red flag! How had I missed that?

We enjoyed an elegant birthday meal with celebratory champagne, and she thanked me for taking her out on her birthday. I asked her how long she would keep up the spoof about my birthday. She sincerely asked me what I was talking about. We stared at each other, completely nonplussed.

After asserting back and forth that today was our birthday, we resorted to showing each other our driver's licenses. Lo and behold, we shared a birthday – precisely ten years apart! I had no idea she was ten years older than me. No wonder she thought of me as a boy toy! The Asian woman stereotype proved itself again.

Holy smokes, as much as I enjoyed her and that my intentions were sincere, she was not a candidate for marriage. As I was on a mission, I politely moved on. I love her to this day.

How many red flags will you ignore?

Some red flags may be acceptable, as the *cost of doing business,* but "don't be no fool."

Red Flags

Dating Red Flags

Avoid these women:

- Daddy issues
- Feminists
- Masculine behavior
- Says she understands men

- Unhappy
- Unlucky
- "deals with" men
- "don't need no man"
- "strong, independent woman"
- Has a master's degree
- Domineering
- Overbearing
- Critical
- Bossy
- Disrespectful
- Spiteful
- Talks about equity
- Believes in a wage gap
- Believes men can get pregnant
- Active ex-boyfriends
- Large debt
- Violent
- Emotional outbursts
- Yelling
- Extreme Jealousy
- Drama queen
- Party girl
- Tattoos and piercings
- Smokes

- High drug use

- High body count

- Low self-esteem

- Frequent job turnover

- Single moms

- Social media addicts

- In charge of birth control

- Chronic illness

- Family drama

- Lack of physical fitness

- Extreme religious commitment

- Sugar babies

- Ungrateful

- Addictive tendencies

- Pathological liars

Avoid these men:

- Abusive
  - Mentally
  - Physically
  - Psychologically

- Lazy
- Possessive
- Controlling
- Domineering
- Manipulative
- Deceitful
- Secretive
- Impatient
- Superficial
- Jealous
- Melodramatic
- Paranoid
- Insecure
- Nice guys
- Wimps
- Simps
- Symps
- Feminists
- Financially unstable
- Unhealthy
- Unfit
- Potheads
- Dangerous sports
- Bad listeners

- Dislikes kids and dogs
- Dresses better than you do
- Lives with parents
- Arrogant
- Intolerant
- Insensitive
- Self-centered
- Greedy
- Miserly
- Pessimistic
- Dishonest
- Unreliable
- Unpredictable
- Envious

Heads up: there are two general types of female prospect.

I don't need no man:

- Liberated
- Overpowering
- Fights for control
- Ignores his needs
- Physically strikes him
- "Going back and forth"

- Disagreeable
- Contrary
- Interruptive
- Uncooperative
- Disrespectful
- Instructional
- Parental
- Superior
- Argumentative
- Competitive
- Confrontational
- Combative
- Independent
- Having the last word
- Smart mouth
- Unfiltered thoughts
- Say they can live without you
- Demands independence
- Makes decisions without consulting
- Demands "equality"
- Corrects him
- Talks over him
- Demands he listen

- Assigns tasks around the home
- Questions his activities
- Demands explanations
- Denies what she has said and done
- Wants to be in charge
- Doubting

I need a man:

- Provides peace
- Is submissive
- Consistently feminine
- Honoring
- Respectful
- Calm
- Peer to peer
- Collaborative
- Dependable
- Cooperative
- Reliable
- Femininity
- Softness
- Gentleness
- Warmth

- Love
- Acknowledgment
- Nurturing
- Appreciative
- Makes him feel needed
- Trusting
- Loyal

Conclusion: know your prospect.

Chapter 2 The Engagement Period

Engagement: Short or long?

- Is the engagement a trial run at marriage?
- Are you engaged because you dated for too long?
- Would it be okay just to be engaged indefinitely?
- What are you engaged for?
- Social correctness?
- More than just dating?
- Are you thinking about getting married?
- Is engagement a logistical bridge to getting married?
- Off the market just long enough to set up a wedding and get married ASAP?
- Are you engaged to let the world know that you are an official couple and will be married soon?

Courtship Deception

Be careful that you really do know each other.

In our eagerness to be together and have our partner appreciate us, we may happily participate in activities we do not intend to adopt as a long-term lifestyle. He may love backpacking, and while she cheerfully went along a couple of times, she will probably never go again. But he doesn't know that. He thinks he has the ideal outdoorsy woman of his dreams. But he doesn't.

She loves the theater and Broadway shows. While they were dating, he went with her to shows two or three times. He enjoyed it as a novel experience but will probably never go again. She doesn't know this. She is thrilled and thinks she has a lifetime buddy to pursue her interests in stage show performances. But she doesn't.

When getting to know each other, we *put our best foot forward*. Is this a form of deception? Perhaps.

We want to stack the deck in favor of better outcomes, but we may not be able to sustain a serious deviation from who we really are.

Long engagements make sense analytically. You can get to know each other and be sure the relationship works.

On the other hand, if it takes a very long time to figure out a relationship, it is probably not right.

Viability should be evident early on. If not clearly viable, time is wasting. Move on. Next!

The woman wants a ring; if she is right for you, put a ring on her finger; take her off the market.

Public or private proposal? That is up to personal taste, but make the event memorable.

"When you realize you want to spend the rest of your life with somebody, you want the rest of your life to start as soon as possible."
~ When Harry Met Sally

"It's been so long now;
But it seems that it was only yesterday.
Gee, ain't it funny
How time slips away?"
~Willie Nelsen

Strategic Dating

"A goal is a broad primary outcome. A strategy is the approach you take to achieve a goal. An objective is a measurable step you take to achieve a strategy. A tactic is a tool you use in pursuing an objective associated with a strategy."
~Mikal E. Belicove
Magazine columnist, Author

Goals, Strategy, Objectives, Tactics

Goals: (Intangible, unmeasurable)

- Productive, lifetime marriage

- Strong, well-paid career path

- Healthy, wholesome family

- **Strategies: (General**

actions)

- Improving yourself to be a good spouse

- Building your career and income

- Approach to achieving a goal

Objectives: (defined, targeted, deadlined)

- Become affluent
- Become influential

- Occupy a strong social position

- Define what is "suitable" for a spouse.

- Determine projected lifestyle factors:

  - Status

  - Location

  - Position

  - Activities

  - Values

- Projected optimum career path

- Targeted training and schooling

- Offspring count

- Projected viable timelines

- Measuring up to the suitable marital candidate

Tactics: (Specific actions, pursuits, activities)

- Employ a matchmaker

- Wardrobe consultant

- Speech and grammar instruction

  - No accents

  - Proper grammar

  - Vocabulary building

  - Public speaking training

- Etiquette coach

- Personal trainer

- Work your ass off

- Be useful

- Get results

- Be reliable

Failure to Launch

Some singles shop and prepare for too long. Some people endlessly hesitate and fail to launch. At some point, a strategic risk will need to be taken. Time is ticking by, especially for women who hope to be mothers. No arrangement will be perfect. *More than adequate* is what you say yes to.

The questions I want you to address:

- Can you find a good enough candidate with whom to risk marriage?
- Can you afford engagement, wedding, and marriage?
- Would you be better off not getting married?
- What makes you think your odds for a lifetime marriage are better than the statistics?
- Will your marriage be for better or for worse?

Chapter 3 Marriage

"Life is a bitch

And then you get married."

~Bert Wolfe

"Check one:

     ○   *With this ring, I go broke.*

     ○   *With this ring, we get rich."*

~Bert Wolfe

"Who you choose to marry is the most important financial decision you will ever make."

~Bert Wolfe

Your Business Partner

The business of life is serious business, and your mate is your business partner in the business of life. Choose wisely.

An Evenly Yoked Marriage

The most critical consideration in a good marriage is that the partners be *evenly yoked*. Evenly yoked is an old-time expression referring to harnessing a pair of oxen to pull a heavy wagon. Observably, an uneven team will struggle compared to an evenly yoked team.

Evenly yoked refers to the married couple having similar values, intelligence, ambitions, and drive.

Once the team is established, leadership must come into play. The woman must be capable of leading in emergencies, but under normal day-to-day circumstances, the husband must lead while the wife is agreeable, cooperative, and supportive. Obviously, there will be exceptions, but five thousand years of human history demonstrate that men generally lead and women support.

Avoid the *Fair-Weather* Lover

It is easy to sustain being *all in love* for a year or two, but maintaining a viable relationship for years on end is a whole nother deal.

It is "good" advice to be engaged for at least five years before getting married. After five years, you will have gotten through *thickness and thin* together - or not.

On the other hand, long engagements may be wimpy wastes of time. For God's sake, if it takes years to determine your prospective mate's suitability for a lifelong marriage, you are probably on the wrong track, wasting valuable marriage-building time.

Your relationship should generate enough power to make your potential look evident to everyone. If not, well, fish or cut bait.

We don't have enough time to waste – especially women who want babies.

So, the goal seems to be to find a solid lifetime mate as soon as possible.

"Who you choose to marry is the most crucial decision you will make in your lifetime."

~Bert Wolfe

What skills and habits will your spouse bring to the business of marriage?

- Good sense and good habits with money?
- Little sense of budgets or spending limits?
- Lives within means?
- Lives *paycheck to paycheck?*
- Expects to be *kept?*
- Wants to be a *homemaker?*
- Makes good money?
- Overspends?
- Saves for the future?

- Consistent and predictable?

- They promise to provide sex?

- They promise to work for good money?

- Wants to make lots of babies?

- Wants to pursue a career?

- Seems to have lots of problems?

- Problem solver?

This list could be pages long. You get the idea.

Who you choose to marry is the most crucial decision you will make in your lifetime.

"One can be attracted to and fall in love with any number of people. So, select wisely."

~Bert Wolfe

Falling in Love

The euphoria of falling in love is like no drug on earth. But like a drug, love can make you do foolish things.

"All you need is love." False! It may be the starting point, but a successful marriage requires far more than love.

You could work your entire adult life and then lose your marriage and all you have built.

Losing love is horrible.

Medical science will never cure the misery of heart sickness or the terrible pain of a broken heart.

But in addition to a broken heart, you will have broken bank accounts and broken dreams.

Love and marriage are rollercoaster rides - plenty of ups and downs.

Marriage can bring your whole life into perfect focus or blow it up.

Marriage can be heaven or hell, or more likely, heaven and hell.

Being *totally in love* is not enough reason to get married. Without careful consideration, don't start signing significant long-term financial commitments to car loans, mortgages, appliance purchases, career changes, etc.

Based on divorce stats, we wonder why anyone ever gets married at all.

And yet, pretty much everybody gets married at some point – even repeatedly.

It seems that humans are hardwired to get married.

What if we could beat the odds and pull off a successful marriage?

Stack the Deck

How could a person *stack the deck* to increase the odds of success in marriage?

Think, plan, and choose wisely.

If you get it reasonably right, call it good and build from there.

Deciding who <u>not</u> to marry can be agonizing when you are *all in love* with an unfunctional candidate. There may be enough magnetism involved to make it painful to part ways. But part ways you must. We don't live for four hundred years.

If you get it wrong, cut your losses without delay. Figure out where you went wrong, make a new plan, and go out and make a better choice.

Enjoy love, but stop senselessly *falling in love*.

Consider the following questions carefully; your life's success and happiness depend on your choices.

Marriage Questions:

- Is marriage really for you?
- What is your purpose for marriage?
- Will you marry at all?
- Why would you get married?
- Is marriage necessary?

- Who will you choose to marry?
- Who will you *not* marry?
- Who will you divest?
- How many times will you marry – trying to get it right?
- Is marriage for you?
- Is marriage a mercenary activity? A pursuit? An accomplishment?
- Is marriage a *rite of passage*?
- Is marriage a status symbol?
- Does it help you feel *established*?
- What would *being married* mean to you?

The only reason to be married is to solidify a powerful soul-to-soul connection with a life partner with similar goals, values, and tastes. Build a spiritual, intellectual marriage. In this modern age, marriage is essentially unnecessary for any other purpose.

For most people, there seems to be a scarcity of available prospective partners. Anxiety about finding someone in time is typically at play. That anxiety is like a toxin; prospects will pick up on it. You must control your desperation and fears not to foul up a good connection.

Be cautious about marrying the first person who will give

you regular sex the way you like. As valuable as that is, it is not the principal reason to marry. Marriage needs to be a complete package.

Some people are quite learned and smart but somehow lack savvy. They make straight As in school but later seem clueless about life's practicalities. This book is especially for them.

I don't know if you should or shouldn't be married or why. I am just saying that you shouldn't be thoughtless and mindless about it. Life is rigorous; only a strong marriage will survive.

Typical reasons people give as benefits of marriage:

- Sex on a regular basis.
- Companionship.
- The economy of sharing expenses.
- Procreation and child-rearing.
- Help when you get old.

Let's keep this simple: *survey says* that these reasons to marry don't reliably bear out.

Non-marriage solutions:

- **Sex on a regular basis:**
  - Dating.
  - Professionals.
- **Companionship**:
  - Go out and make friends.
  - Join clubs and activity groups.
  - Get a dog.
- **The economy of sharing expenses:**
  - Get a roommate you are not sexually involved with.
- **Procreation and child-rearing:**
  - Do you need to do this?
  - Adopt.
  - Join a Big Brother/Big Sister organization.
  - Be a super aunt/uncle.
- **Do your children need you to be married?**
  - No.
  - Odds are, you will be divorced anyway.
- **Help when you get old:**
  - Progressive living facilities.
  - Take care of your health when you are young so you are not broken down when you get old.
  - Earn and keep enough money to pay for your own old age.

Legal Alternatives to Marriage

There are alternatives to marriage for couples who want to commit to each other without getting legally married. Some common ones are:

- **Domestic partnership**: provides some of the rights and benefits of marriage, such as inheritance, hospital visitation, healthcare directives, and health insurance benefits.

- **Common law marriage**: recognizes a couple as married if they live together for a certain period and present themselves as married to others. If you want to avoid the consequences of legal marriage, show no evidence of cohabitation by keeping your bills and addresses entirely separate. If not managed carefully, one could be successfully sued for a divorce settlement.

- **Cohabitation agreement**: a contract that outlines the rights and obligations of living together without marriage. Cohabitation agreements cover property, finances, children, inheritance, healthcare directives, and hospital access.

- **Religious marriage**: Married "in the eyes of the church" and subject to the conventions of that tradition. Statutory authorities may not recognize a religious marriage.

These are possible alternatives to government marriage. Nevertheless, these agreements are fundamentally legal instruments, so the government and the legal system may still become involved. When people couple up, it is nearly impossible to avoid legal entanglements. It seems that legal entanglements are simply part of the deal, so "everybody" does it.

Prenuptial Agreements

A prenuptial agreement could protect assets owned before the marital union occurs. A prenuptial agreement can address property division, previously held assets, debts, children, pets, and tax filing status.

It determines the rights of each spouse at the time of divorce. Are they worth the paper they are written on? Perhaps, sometimes, maybe, if drawn up correctly. Detailed rules and conditions apply, and expert legal advice is required. Different jurisdictions have different rules.

A court could void a prenuptial agreement for several reasons:

- Unconscionable unfairness
- Failure to disclose financial details or hidden assets
- Duress, pressure, or coercion
- Fraud or false promises
- Inadequate spousal support limits
- Not represented by a separate attorney or waived the right

A prenuptial agreement that includes sex may be considered a sex contract. You generally can't contract for sex, whether it is for money or a requirement of marriage. The theory is that a sex contract deprives an individual of the right to control their body. If enforceable, a sex contract would penalize a person for refusing to fulfill the contract. Yet, how is this different from any service or employment contract? The service provider is expected to use their body to perform work. Isn't that the purpose of an enforceable agreement or contract that there will be delineated consequences for failure to fulfill specified services?

Many would contend that access to regular sex is the fundamental basis of marriage. Without the implied sexual contract, few men would ever marry. So, by logic, marriage is innately a sex contract.

It seems that society finds it unacceptable to "spell out" a sexual contract – even in the context of marriage.

What is the remedy for implicit obligations that are disregarded and not being met?

Time, Sex, and Money

Any marital counselor will confirm that couples fight about sex and money. Typically, he is frustrated that she doesn't give him enough sex and respect, while she is frustrated that he doesn't make enough money, doesn't listen enough, and doesn't give her enough attention.

- Fighting couples don't enjoy marriage.
- Fighting couples don't make ideal parents.
- Fighting couples usually get divorced.
- Divorced couples don't make ideal parents.

Typical Scenario: Married couples spend fantastically more money living together than two non-married roommates will. The married woman wants to *feather* her marital nest and show it off pridefully. The man typically wants expensive toys. The couple wants to appear successful, so they spend too much on furniture, travel, and cars. There is often speculative investing at too early a stage in their life. Putting on a good show is costly. Pretty soon, there will be babies in the nest. The husband may struggle to keep up with the show's expenses. The wife may begin complaining about their rate of success. She may also start complaining about her husband's state of anxiety.

Generally speaking, the woman has already closed the deal by achieving marriage, so her incentive to provide sex diminishes. The husband becomes sexually frustrated, and his frustration turns into chronic anxiety. Chronic anxiety comes across as "anger." This is the classic recipe for divorce. Typically, the wife thinks it is her job to improve conditions in all categories, including him. Since the wife chronically observes non-optimum situations, she makes comments and suggestions. To the husband, this can look like nitpicking criticism. The wife will appear dissatisfied as she quests to improve everything around her. The man will become defensive and anxious about "failing" to get everything right. The man will interpret a lack of sex as his failure to satisfy his woman. The diminished sexual activity, combined with his feeling criticized for not making enough money, not dressing right, and saying wrong things, etc., will lead the man to conclude that he is failing in his marriage.

Now, the man is working as much overtime as he can. Unless the mother is very well paid, her commuting and childcare expenses cannot be justified, so she stays home earning no money.

There are exceptions to this pattern and millions of variations, but this is arguably the typical pattern.

The significant shortages in marriage are time, sex, and money. There never seems to be enough time for physical intimacy, and your job will use up all the time you let it.

Look it up: the divorce rate in America is well beyond 50%; therefore, the odds of being with your current spouse in old age are poor.

You will look back and see that more dollars could have been stashed. More could have been spent on professional training and education and adventure travel.

Fancy Expenses Too Early:

- Fancy clothes, watches, and jewelry
- Fancy cars
- Fancy furniture and home décor
- Fancy yard and deck
- Fancy renovations
- Fancy vacations
- Fancy memberships
- Fancy investments
- Fancy wine and liquor, and cigars
- Fancy electronics
- Fancy debt

Marriage is More Than Just One Simple Relationship

A married couple will share several relationship roles within the context of marriage, and each role is essential and must not be ignored. The triggers to a divorce are typically some combination of disagreeing about money, sex, and how to raise the kids.

Individual Roles of a Marriage Partnership:

- Business Partner
- Roommate
- Companion
- Lover
- Conversationalist
- Friend
- Travel partner
- Child parent
- Pet parent
- Home owner

Relative accord in each role must be maintained to sustain a marriage.

I have specifically observed divorces caused by:

- Disagreements about money.
- Disagreements about how to manage and raise children.
- Sexual disharmony.
- Disagreements about how to keep the house.
- Lack of *conversation*.
- Disrespect.
- Physical and/or emotional abuse.
- Lack of sleep.
- Drug and alcohol abuse.

Each of these could lead to divorce. Don't kid yourself about this. If there are any two disharmonies, you will be divorced. Work this shit out. If you are caught up in an irreparably dysfunctional marriage, get out as soon as possible. Time is wasting. The sand is fast running out of your hourglass.

"Most people believe that you marry the person with whom you "fall in love." Like a "one and only." Most people have not considered how many kinds of marriage there are. If you look around, you will see them."

~Bert Wolfe

Many types of marriage:

- Marriage of Love

- Marriage of Affection

- Great Love

- Marriage of Familiarity

- Marriage of Mutual Attraction

- Marriage of Beauty

- Glamour Marriage

- Marriage of Lust

- Family Marriage

- Clan Marriage

- Strategic Marriage

- Problem-Solving Marriage

- Marriage for Children
- Business Marriage

- Strategic Marriage

- Enterprise Marriage

- Marriage for Power

- Marriage for Image

- Marriage of Convenience

- Marriage to Escape

- Marriage of Guilt

- Socialite Marriage

- Career Marriage

- Intellectual Marriage

- Higher Purpose Marriage

- Travel Marriage
- Sports Marriage
- Fun Marriage
- Mutual Hobby Marriage
- Altruism Marriage
- Political Marriage
- Common Interest Marriage
- Intellectual Marriage
- Pet/Animal Marriage
- Conversational Marriage
- Mutual Admiration and Respect
- Soul Mates

"The brain is an outstanding organ. It works for 24 hours, 365 days, right from birth until you fall in love."

~Unknown

"For God's sake, whatever you do, don't fall in love!"

~T. F. Weird

Artist/Philosopher

Falling in Love

Falling in love can be a gravity sport, and it can be thrilling; however, *falling* sometimes results in traumatic injuries. The old joke is, "It's not the falling that hurts; it's the landing." So, be careful about falling in love. Falling in love can be very exciting, but it is serious business. Falling in love can lead to all kinds of dysfunctional shenanigans. Falling in love often leads to broken hearts, damaged souls, and depleted bank accounts. Most of the time, "falling in love" is more like *falling in lust*. Lust is fun and exciting, but it may not be the best foundation for a long-term successful marriage.

Sane Alternates to *Falling* in Love:

- Finding love
- Discovering love
- Developing love
- Building love
- Arranging love
- Creating love
- Choosing love
- Mutual love

What do we mean by love anyway? We think we marry for love, but what kind of love? Various types of love can be fun, exciting, and satisfying.

"Sanskrit has 96 words for love; ancient Persian has 80, Greek three, and English only one. This is indicative of the poverty of awareness or emphasis that we give to that tremendously important realm of feeling. Eskimos have 30 words for snow because it is a life-and-death matter to them to have exact information about the element they live with so intimately. If we had a vocabulary of 30 words for love, we would immediately be richer and more intelligent in this human element so close to our hearts.

An Eskimo probably would die of clumsiness if he had only one word for snow; we are close to dying of loneliness because we have only one word for love. Of all the Western languages, English may be the most lacking when it comes to feeling."

~Robert Johnson
The Fisher King and the Handless Maiden

Intense Love

Both can love intensely. But, generally, men experience more intense love. The reason may be that there aren't enough men around that women consider worthy of intense love. Most men can intensely love an ordinary woman.

A psychologist from Pennsylvania State University, Marissa Harrison, believes that women are more cautious about relationships, while men fall in love harder and faster.

"Me and Loretta, we don't talk much anymore.

She sits and stares through the back door screen.

And all the news just repeats itself.
Like some forgotten dream that we've both seen.'

~John Prine

Hello in There

Conversation

A while back, I was dismayed that a longtime couple from my parents' generation was getting divorced. Their kids were through college, fully raised, and on their own. The divorcing couple had become complete *empty-nesters*. So far, they had no grandchildren, so it seemed they had lost enough common purpose and personal connection to have drifted far apart. One of their contemporary friends said: "They no longer had *conversation*." They had lost their *conversation*, which was the marriage's end.

There are all kinds of marriages, not just one "fell in love" kind of marriage.

Attention, Admiration, Respect

"Admiration and respect are the basis of enduring love."

~**Bert Wolfe**

"Women need admiration and love while men need respect."

~Bert Wolfe

Attention and admiration

Attention and admiration go together, but they are not the same thing. Attention is when someone takes notice of another as interesting or important and deserving of special care. Admiration is more like respect and warm approval; The loved one is admired as impressive or worthy of respect.

A husband could give his wife a lot of attention and fail to admire her. He could also admire her and yet fail to give her enough attention. Some exquisite balance is needed to maintain harmony. This balance is an undefined x-factor that requires careful conscious effort.

"Attention is like wind; the woman is like a sailboat. If the wind stops, the sailboat loses direction and drifts away."

~J. D. Rose

"Attention is like sunlight; it makes things grow, and when it stops,

things die in the dark."

~J. D. Rose

Standing In Love

"Love is not just a passion spark between two people; there is an infinite difference between falling in love and standing in love. Rather, love is a way of being, a 'giving to' not a 'falling for;' a mode of relating at large, not an act limited to a single person."

Dr, Irvin Yalom
Psychiatry Guru

Common types of sad marriages:

- Marriage of Resignation
- Disharmonious Marriage
- Coping Marriage
- Marriage of Boredom
- "Lots have been Cast" Marriage
- Exhausted Marriage
- Apathetic Marriage
- Worn out Marriage
- Angry Marriage
- Bickering Marriage
- Argumentative Marriage
- Contradictory Marriage
- Conflicting Goals Marriage
- Dream Killing Marriage
- Marriage of Fear

- Marriage of Obligation
- Marriage of Habit
- Sexless Marriage
- Plodding Marriage
- Poverty Marriage
- Marriage of Guilt
- Going Through the Motions
- Marriage of Indebtedness
- Sad Marriage

Presumably, these couples had been *in love* in the beginning.

Most people careen through life, making random choices based on *instinct* and happenstance.

What if you developed some basic guidelines and a general plan that focused your choices toward better outcomes?

Contract Creep

The practical reality is that a marriage is inherently and fundamentally a business partnership. The couple starts with a legal "marriage contract." The couple progressively takes on (signs) more and more legal contracts - contracts for loans and services. It seems that the primary activity of marriage is to manage serious debt. And typically, the debt structure is complicated. And these are not individual contractual obligations; they are co-signed partnership obligations. Over time, "contract creep" takes over. Most couples have never stopped to consider the layers of legally binding contracts they have piled on over the years.

Typical Contracts of Marriage Obligation

- Marriage contract
- Apartment lease
- House mortgage
- Automobile lease
- Automobile purchase loan
- Furniture and appliance loans
- Homeowners' insurance
- Automobile insurance
- Child one
- Child two
- Child three
- Joint bank accounts
- Business loans
- Lines of credit
- Service contracts
- Shared credit cards
- Retirement accounts
- Annuities
- Lines of credit
- Partnerships

- Incorporations, LLCs, trusts
- Purchase and sale agreements
- Insurance beneficiary assignments
- Investment loans
- Joint retirement accounts
- Second home loans
- Reverse mortgages
- Healthcare directives
- Living wills
- Last wills and testaments

Are you sure you want to entangle yourself with someone else to this extreme extent?

If so, really, why?

Don't ever say, "I didn't warn you."

So, again, you will almost certainly get married – choose wisely.

Advice: Have your prospective mate read this book.

Ambiguous advice: Marry later in life; you will be older and wiser. You will have gained experience of your own, and you will have observed others. Over time, you may gain wisdom to apply to a more mature relationship. **On the other hand,** time is wasting. Get well married as soon as possible.

"The divorce rate for a first marriage in America is 40-50%. After a first divorce, the common assumption is that a second marriage will fare better from previously learned experience. The divorce rate for a second marriage is 60-67%. Although many people who have divorced twice continue to marry again, the success rates are not in their favor. The divorce rate for a third marriage increases to roughly 70%."

~Rebecca Lee

Recipe for Divorce:

- Poor spouse choice
- Married too young
- Too many children too early
- Too little sex
- Too much house too soon
- Job and career hopping
- Long commutes are getting longer
- Excessive automobile expense
- Overspending
- Not enough money
- Alcohol and drug abuse
- Unbalanced lifestyle

Why do so many marriages fail?

What goes wrong?

How do we make it go right?

There are hundreds of books on the subject.

Failure to understand our primal roles may be to blame. It is critical to understand that men build and women nurture. Men build, maintain, expand, and protect the infrastructures of life. Women create and nurture offspring, the future of the race.

"Her purpose is the creation of the human race. The female of the race is responsible for its tomorrow."

~J. D. Rose

"Men build, maintain, expand, and protect the infrastructures of life. Women create and nurture offspring, the future of the race."

~Bert Wolfe

"Action is relatively more effective in provision and defense while talking is more effective in raising children."

~J. D. Rose

"Here is your husband's greatest fear:

He is afraid of disappointing you.

Actually, he is afraid of being a disappointment. "

~Justin Davis

"Many women's worst fear is aging, ending up alone,

penniless, and on the street. There's even a term for it—

bag lady syndrome. "

~ Justin Davis

"Women fear dying broke and alone. A man fears failing

to provide adequately for his wife and family. Ironically,

divorce is the ultimate expression of both spouses' fears.

Divorce proves both fears to be real. Commitment and

loyalty are the solution to divorce. Women need to commit

themselves to loyalty, and men need to work their asses

off and provide for the family. "

~ Bert Wolfe

Big news: men and women are different.

- Men Build
- Women Nurture

A cruel god designed husbands and wives to be so

different. And, most cruel, to provide no manual. "

~Bert Wolfe

The Rings of Suffering:

- Class ring
- Promise ring
- Engagement ring
- Wedding ring
- Nose ring
- Suffering

Sexual Compatibility

Viable sexual compatibility is crucial in dating and leads to the decision to marry, whereas sexual compatibility often changes after marriage. Viable sexual compatibility is essential to maintaining a lifetime marriage.

Men have different sexual needs and desires than women. Men's need for sex may be physical and driven by testosterone. His intimacy needs may be different as well; sexual connection may be necessary for men to feel ready for emotional vulnerability.

Generally speaking, women require romance and intimacy to prime them for sex, while men need sex to get to intimacy and bonding.

Husbands

Sexuality for married men is different from the sexuality of single men.

Generally speaking, single men will simply go without sex or find a way to get it when they need it. Single men don't tend to build up the frustrations that married men can. Married men will likely become sexually frustrated if they have insufficient sex because they expect and believe the marriage contract assures them regular sexual release (relief). To make things much worse for the married man, his chosen sexual partner is always around, arousing his sexual interest – with her pheromones, lingerie, and unique attractiveness that makes him desire her. A single man would never share a bed with a woman who wouldn't let him have sex. For a husband, a chaste marital bed is a torture chamber.

Married men get to intimacy through sex. Without sex, husbands feel isolated, lonely, and unappreciated. If sex is delayed or denied, anxiety will start building up in the husband. He will become distant and edgy in interactions.

He will begin to feel burned out and unmotivated. He will withdraw. If this anxiety builds for too long, he will become frustrated. His frustration will look and feel like anger to his wife. When a husband gets horny enough, it is almost impossible to generate a romantic connection before he has sex. If marital sex has been forestalled, the man will have a demanding, almost desperate, pent-up need that will supersede romance and tenderness. When the husband finally gets some sex, he will still be pent-up and out of balance. The wife may find this kind of sex rather perfunctory and lacking in romance and tenderness. The husband can't get to the romance when his frustration is too intense. Once the frustration is quenched, the man typically feels intimate and bonded with his wife again. His endocrine and nervous systems will be rebalanced and calmed. She may rebuff his post-coital gestures of intimacy because she didn't get romance first. He will be hurt and offended that she doesn't feel close now – while he does. This pattern becomes a heartbreaking dwindling spiral toward romantic and sexual estrangement.

For husbands, the marital contract is supposed to assure loyalty, respect, and regular sex. If a wife fails in this regard, the marriage fails.

The classic old joke for long-time married couples goes like this:

"We only have hallway sex now."

"When we pass each other in the hallway, we say, fuck you to each other."

Another classic joke:

"We have Social Security sex; we get a little each month, but not enough to live on."

Wives

Single women only have sex when they feel like it. Generally speaking, women don't have the overwhelming need for regular sex that men do. Single women don't have the contractual obligation to provide sex to a partner regularly. While a wife may enjoy sex very much, she may not have the powerful biological imperative to have sex as frequently as husbands do.

So, a wife may find herself burdened with the need to provide sex more frequently than what was natural to her as a single woman.

Wives get to sex through intimacy. Without some romance and intimacy, a woman is disinclined to provide sex. She will feel unloved and used somehow and become owly and unpleasant if she doesn't get the attention she needs before sex. She will create distance in her demeanor. If a woman goes long enough without the attention and appreciation she needs, she may find it psychologically challenging to provide sex.

For wives, the marital contract is supposed to provide them with a dedicated, attentive listener, a man to help protect and feather her nest, and a husband to help her put on her show. The husband must listen attentively, have good grooming, and help her coordinate her presentation to the world.

Dissimilar Needs for Attention:

- Wives and husbands also have different needs for getting attention from one another. These needs may seem simplistic and immature to both parties, but don't disregard them; they are powerfully universal.

- The wife needs her husband to assure her that she is attractive to him and amazing at putting on her unique show. She needs companionship and for him to listen to her – a lot.

- The husband needs to feel that she thinks he is cool. And that his interests and what he does for a living are vital and fundamentally *cool*. The wife must decide that his stuff is cool and valid.

- The husband needs regular sexual intimacy.

The fundamental jobs:

- The **husband's job** is to protect his wife and make her feel important, beautiful, and amazing. A woman wants companionship, and a woman wants admiration. So, give her lots of both.

- The **wife's job** is to acknowledge that he is capable and cool. A man requires respect.

The critical rules of engagement:

The Husband

- He must support the wife's show even if he privately feels it is silly or superficial. He must admire how well she gets everything *right* and help her get it more right.
- If she asks him to help her with the show, he must appreciate the *worthiness* of the endeavor, consider it valid, and make no disparaging comments.
- The husband should never try to teach the wife anything and avoid explaining anything to her.
- He needs to listen to her – a lot.
- The husband must create and provide romance and intimacy.

The Wife

- She must believe he is indispensable and very cool.
- The wife must never belittle the husband's efforts – even if the efforts are less than adequate.
- The wife must never indicate that he has nerdish or childish interests or activities – even though she may have little personal interest in his *cool* activities.
- When the wife asks the husband to do something for her, she must tell him when she wants it done and how she wants it to turn out. However, the wife must never tell the husband how to do anything.

- The wife must provide unbegrudging sex on a regular as-needed basis.

It is as Simple as That

It's pretty much just that simple. There are millions of variations in millions of marriages, but confusion about each other's roles is the most fundamental reason marriages break down.

A cruel god designed husbands and wives to be so different. And, most cruelly, not to provide a manual.

Long-term success involves a management pattern that satisfies both the husband and the wife enough to sustain the union. One might think that the colossal cost of divorce is sufficient to motivate a couple to provide for each other. I believe the catastrophic divorce rate in America is more due to the mutual ignorance of the nature of husbands and wives than to some stubborn unwillingness to provide for each other. I contend that most married couples have little comprehension of the differences in the needs of their partners. A fundamentally loving couple that understands each other's needs will happily provide for each other.

Realistically, most humans never feel fully satisfied, but only briefly. The best we can achieve is feeling mostly satisfied most of the time, but it's upsetting to feel chronically dissatisfied.

It is essential to understand that dissatisfaction is valuable and fuels a powerful human drive to reach more optimal conditions. However, chronic dissatisfaction ruins life; anxiety and frustration can become overwhelming. To be reasonably happy, we need to balance satisfaction and dissatisfaction.

"A fundamentally loving couple that understands each other's needs will happily provide for each other."

~Bert Wolfe

Cardinal Sins

Her mistakes:

- Buzz-killing a man's enjoyment.
- Comparing him negatively to either of his parents.
- Raising her voice.
- Verbal abuse.
- Ridiculing his cool hobbies.
- Undermining his "cool" in any way.
- Making fun of his cool personal interests. *Thereby showing him disrespect.*
- Digging up the past to rub his face in.
- Withholding sex.
- Weaponizing sex.
- Trading sex as a commodity.

His mistakes:

- Failing to listen to her feelings long enough and carefully enough.

- Trying to solve her emotional issues.

- Failing to admire her openly.

- Failing to create romance.

- Failing to be tender and chivalrous.

- Making fun of her efforts to make everything just right.

- Ridiculing her for keeping the nest feathered just so.

- Undermining her show in any way. (Thereby failing to admire how uniquely special she is.)

- Failing to do the *heavy lifting* for her show.

- Failing to protect her, the nest, and any babies in the nest.

- Failing to sufficiently "provide."

- Comparing her negatively to either of her parents.

- Any physical abuse.

- Gaslighting.

"So, pay attention. If it's important to her, it is important to you. If you don't believe me, you will suffer."

~J. D. Rose

Classic joke: A majority of archeologists are women due to their natural ability to dig up the past.

"71% of archaeologists are female and 29% are male."

~Career Explorer

What about Sex?

"Absence makes the heart grow fonder; presence makes the libido grow stronger."

~Bert Wolfe

Marital Sex Inquiry

Is having sex:

- A rare event?
- An awkward affair?
- A celebration?
- Spontaneous?
- Fun?
- A special occasion?
- Orchestrated?
- A normal routine?
- A special routine?
- A scheduled event?
- Pre-arranged?

Healthy feelings to look for when you think about your mate:

- Appreciation
- Admiration
- Attraction
- Respect
- Comfort
- Gratitude
- Warmth
- Softness
- Tingles
- Trust
- Safety
- Confidence
- Awe
- Joy
- Stability
- Security
- Contentment
- Fulfillment

Positives of a Good Marriage

- Stabile financial partnership
- Mutual trust
- Watching over each other's health
- Companionship
- Physical intimacy
- Shared bonding experiences
- Mutual goals

Arranged Marriage

By all reports, *arranged marriages* have remarkable success rates. Typical Americans find the idea of someone else arranging their marriage to be abhorrent. But how about if you consciously and strategically *arrange* your own marriage?

Friendship

The ultimate goal of marriage might be genuine friendship. However, I don't think friendship is a given in marriage. Companionship might be more common. Friendship takes time and events to build the bond.

I often hear, "My spouse is my best friend." I just can't see that as viable. Marital partners have too much at stake to maintain mutual "best friend" status. Presumably, a best friend would be a nonjudgmental confidant. I see that role as nearly impossible for marital partners. It makes no sense to "bare it all" to your marital partner. A man should definitely never *bear it all* emotionally to a woman; he would lose face irreparably. And if a woman *bared it all* to a man, well, he probably could take it emotionally, but he wouldn't like it.

Wives are hardwired to fix up their husbands. Husbands don't want to be improved. Men don't want to know a woman's secrets. Spouses trying to be best friends is a total conflict of interests.

A safe, intimate friendship would be the highest goal of marriage.

Best friends are sourced outside the marriage and are of the same gender.

With rare exceptions, a best friend, by nature, needs to be the same gender as you. Opposite genders can never fully understand each other.

Conclusion: On paper, I cannot recommend marriage, but since pretty much everybody does it, make sure you will beat the odds. This book is about thinking before choosing and following plans and personal policies.

Do not get married on a whim. Marriage is serious business, financially. Build a marriage that will last. Hard work is to be expected. Lasting marriages survive on sheer force of will.

Chapter 4 Lasting Marriage

"If I get married, I want to be very married."

~Audrey Hepburn

"The most fundamental goal of marriage is to obtain, retain, and remain."

~Bert Wolfe

"If you choose to marry, make marriage a lifetime commitment. Financially speaking, a marriage must be a lifelong commitment."

~Bert Wolfe

"Without loyalty and commitment, your marriage will not last."

~Bert Wolfe

"People say, oh, relationships are tough. No, they not; they're only tough when one person's working on it. Twopeople can move a couch real easy; one person can't move it at all."

~Chris Rock

"If you are in a relationship, let me try to help you right now. Rule one: stop competing. Her success is your success, and your success is her success. Number two: there is no equality in a relationship. You are both there to serve; you are in the service industry."

"You are in a band. In a band, you have roles that you play in the band. Sometimes you sing lead, and sometimes you're on tambourine. And if you are on tambourine, play it right; play it with a fucking smile because nobody wants to see a mad tambourine player."

~Chris Rock

"Marriage is not a noun; it's a verb. It isn't something you get. It's something you do. It's the way you love your partner every day."

~Barbara De Angelis

Love is a Verb

Use the word love as a verb, like you use the word work as a verb. Love is work. So, get to love, put your love in, love hard, and love with discipline. Show up for love early and love late. Love overtime. Don't call in sick. Show up for love daily, even when you don't feel like it. You won't feel like going to love every day, but go to love anyway.

Rejection (selfish with sex)

Routinely rejecting sexual advances and romantic intimacy might seem like her prerogative, but marriage is a partnership; if you only want to do things only when you feel like it, you should be single.

Sometimes, a partner will selfishly withhold sex and only offer it when they feel like it. In marriage, partners do all kinds of things for each other when it is inconvenient because it makes their partner feel loved.

If a husband is no longer all over her, grabbing her ass and watching her undress, it's because she has discouraged him by saying things like "Stop" and "Is that all you think about?"

This backfires into the wife feeling no longer desirable to her husband. His once playfully romantic gestures will quickly be replaced with detached sullenness.

The wife should ask herself which one she would rather have, her husband pestering her sexually or him disregarding her and holding her at a distance.

Does she want to feel sexually desired or, instead, relegated to his indifference?

Consequences of Divorce

The man loses considerably more than half in a divorce. The wife/mother stays in the house with all the furniture, appliances, and accessories. Typically, the man moves to a rental apartment with his toys and the lesser car. The wife/mother's material lifestyle will remain principally the same.

The man will be set back to where he was when he first left his parents' house.

Is this fair? Probably not, but the practicality is that it will nearly always work out this way if children are involved. If you get married and have children, there is roughly a 75% chance that this will happen to you. How will you afford this? How will you start over? What is your plan?

Ingredients of Divorce Loss:

- Real Property (real estate)
- Personal Property
- Retirement accounts
- Investments
- House and home
- Social status
- Living conditions
- Emotional/Psychological condition
- Professional confidence and prowess

Children of Divorce

One of divorce's most significant consequences is its impact on children. Children of divorce are more likely to experience trouble in school, have lousy relationships with their parents, and suffer from emotional and behavioral problems. Studies show that children of divorced parents are more likely to experience depression, anxiety, and low self-esteem. They will struggle with feelings of abandonment, confusion, and anger.

Children whose parents divorced are also more likely to experience poverty, as the family income is reduced after a divorce. Poverty leads to desperation; desperation leads to desperate behavior.

Divorce is a financial disaster, and I would argue that financially successful couples should never divorce. So be it if they must legally separate but never destroy the economic construct. Work something out to preserve your hard-earned capital and financial progress. Set pride aside and work something out; make arrangements; don't get divorced.

What divorce could cost:

- $40K legal fees
- $500K half of the stuff
- $500K half the house
- $10KDating
- $20K career advancement and productivity drop
- $5K Counseling
- **Total: $1,075,000.00**

Don't forget to add "child support" and "alimony" to this

total. You basically have these expenses during marriage, but the vast difference is that you will no longer have the "enjoyment" of your wife and children every day.

Divorce is idiotic; work that shit out.

Commitment

"What is the number 1 reason for divorce? Lack of commitment is the most common reason given by divorcing couples, according to a recent national survey. Here are the reasons given and their percentages: Lack of commitment, 73%; Argue too much, 56%."

wf-lawyers.com

https://www.wf-lawyers.com › divorce-statistics-and-facts

Lack of commitment is the most common reason for divorce. 75% of individuals and couples cite a lack of commitment as the reason for their divorce. Weak commitment is the most common cause of divorce, exceeding infidelity.

Among college-educated couples, the percentage of divorces initiated by wives is 90 percent. Women tend to initiate divorce more than men in all relationships outside of even college-educated couples.

Men and women are wired differently; we need to

understand this.

A Man's Greatest Need

When I ask the general public what a man's greatest need is, they usually say sex, which is probably number two.

The number one thing men need in marriage is <u>loyalty</u>. Men know that women initiate 80% of divorces, and they know they have a 60% chance of getting divorced. There is not one benefit for a man to get married; therefore, **loyalty** is the most important thing a woman can offer.

A Man's Greatest Fear

A man's greatest fear is having a woman take more than half of everything he has worked for, plus his kids, pets, and home. He is terrified that he will be set back to a college lifestyle in middle age and have to rebuild his life. He knows from observing his peers that a divorce setback cannot be fully overcome, and the only way to win financially is never to divorce.

A Woman's Greatest Fear

When I ask the general public what a woman's greatest need is, they usually say love, which is way off the mark. Her greatest fear is poverty and that she will become a homeless bag lady.

It sounds good that a woman's greatest need is love, but that is not even close. Security is a woman's greatest need; after security comes love and admiration.

Women love men based on detailed criteria; *conditional love* belongs to women (*true love* and *blind love* belong to men.) These are not wholesome kinds of love but are observably the most common.

A Woman's Greatest Need

A woman's greatest need is <u>financial and physical security</u>; women turn to men for this.

Husbands' fears:

- Failing to provide for his wife and family
- Being a disappointment
- Not good enough
- Loss of relevance
- Not measuring up
- Not being needed
- Not being lovable
- Rejection
- Divorce
- Humiliation
- Being controlled
- Being smothered
- Being pussy whipped

- Being turned into a pussy
- Being considered a *nice guy*
- Sexless marriage

What men don't like in a relationship:

- Having to check in
- Having to account for their whereabouts
- Reduced *guy* time
- Needing *permission* to do independent activities
- Having their things moved
- Rearranging the house
- Being humiliated
- Dealing with previous men's baggage
- Being compared to other men
- "Girls' night out"
- Dressing sexy to work
- Being denied sex

Things a man loves in his wife:

- Her respect for his leadership, knowledge, and how he provides
- How she looks good for him at home
- Her femininity
- Her competence
- Her lack of masculinity
- How she shows confidence in him and his abilities

- She appreciates his help, his protection, and his tiredness
- She provides peace and quiet
- She speaks well of him to her family and to his family
- He loves her affection and physical touches

Wives' fears:

- Bag Lady Syndrome
- Dying broke and alone
- Destitute on the street
- Being disgraced in front of her peers
- Being abused
- Being partnered with an addict

What wives don't want in a marriage:

- Sexual affairs
- Gambling
- Dangerous sports
- Addiction
- Unstable careers

Men Need to Pay Attention

Classic joke:

Wife: 'You weren't even listening, were you?!

Husband: "That's a strange way to start a conversation."

Anatomy of a classic conflict:

A. The husband fails to *pay attention.*

B. The wife's feelings are hurt.

C. The wife concludes that the husband doesn't care, *is clueless,* or both.

D. For this, the husband will pay!

E. The penalty: the husband is *cut off* from poon, love, and affection.[1]

F. The wife innately knows something is illogical about her emotional conclusions, so she will continue to come home every day to feed her husband.

G. Feeding the husband is a sublimation of her innate urge to serve the husband sexually.

---

[1] "Cut off" symbolically, as in the penis cut off or at least blocked from the vagina.

H. The husband notices that he is being fed but not fed.

I. The wife is feeling dissatisfied by a lack of attention and appreciation.

J. She is unconsciously programmed to believe it is the husband's job to satisfy her.

K. The husband's sexual frustration and anxiety will come across as "anger" to the wife.

L. She will become more recalcitrant.

M. The husband will continue to be clueless about the wrong he has perpetrated.

N. The husband will try to make amends by giving flowers and other propitiative gestures.

O. The gestures will fall short because he doesn't know what he did.

P. The husband may fail even to ask what the problem is because he can't bear another confusing argument.

Q. She won't tell him because he should know without being told.

R. The explanation is held out as a test. (If he really loved me, he would just know.)

S. He is not a mind reader. (He can't know anything without him asking or her telling.).

T. He won't ask. (Because it will lead to more incriminations that he doesn't understand.)

A possible solution to the "Husband fails; Wife

penalizes" problem:

A. Husband musters up the guts to ask, "What is wrong?"

B. Wife tells him.

C. The husband listens ardently without interrupting.

D. Husband gains some understanding of wife's considerations.

E. The husband accepts as much blame as he can bear.

F. The husband assumes accountability.

G. The husband declares that he will work to be a better listener.

H. The husband makes a point of appreciating her exceptional efforts.

I. The husband tells the wife how much he appreciates and admires her above all other women.

J. The wife resumes service to the husband.

K. The wife is acknowledged, and the husband has his needs met.

Something like that.

Commitment

"Until one is committed, there is hesitancy;
The chance to draw back.
Concerning all acts of initiative and creation,
There is one elementary truth,
The ignorance of which kills countless ideas and splendid
plans:That the moment one definitely commits oneself,
Then Providence moves, too.
All sorts of things occur to help one.
That would never otherwise have occurred.
A whole stream of events issues from the decision,
raising in one's favor all manner of unforeseen incidents
and meetings and material assistance,
Which no man could have dreamed would have come his
way. Whatever you can do or dream you can do, begin it.
Boldness has genius, power, and magic in it.
Begin it now."

~ Johan Wolfegang von Goethe

"The ignorance of the mechanics of commitment and the
failure to actively commit kills countless ideas, splendid
plans, and marriages."

~Bert Wolfe

How to Keep a Man

- Demonstrate loyalty
- Stay slim
- Long hair
- Sex anytime
- Talk less
- Provide peace
- Treat him like he is cool
- Do not attempt to *feminize* your man
- Do not *mother* your grown man
- If he takes you out, he gets laid
- If he dresses up, hc gets laid
- If he wears a tuxedo, he gets laid

How to Keep a Woman

- Maintain a high-paying job (the more money and perceived power, the better).
- Create the impression that you are influential.
- Appear to be important to the outside world.
- Be braggable to other women.
- Listen
- Listen a lot
- Listen intently
- Do not problem-solve
- Offer no opinions
- Exhibit no attitude

- Make intermittent, small acknowledgments:
  - "Wow."
  - "Really?"
  - "WTF?"
  - "Unbelievable."
  - "Wow."
  - "Oh my god."
  - "What else?"
  - "Wow!"
  - "That's amazing."
  - "I understand."
  - "I get it."
- Endure until she is finished.

Man rules: Maintain Boundaries; refuse to listen to these topics:

- Gossip
- Superfluous bad news
- Criticism
- Corrections
- Instructions

- No mothering
- Create romance (women crave romance but rarely know how to create it.) (Women want to be seduced.)

Key romantic events:

- Special occasions
- Dress-up events

- Making her laugh without you ever being a clown[2]
- Acts of chivalry
- She sees you admire her
- Support her show
- Never belittle her show
- No sarcasm
- Contribute to the show
- Let her take all the credit
- Look good and act well for her show
- Solve her problems (but never during her talking sessions)

- Good grooming (different from good hygiene)

- Wear contemporary, *high-value-man* clothing
- Wear expensive *power* shoes
- Avoid *metro* clothing and shoes
- Do the heavy lifting

---

[2] No buffoonery

- Actively protect her
- Practice chivalry (do it even if she says she is liberated)
  - Doors
  - Coats
  - Chairs
  - Stairs
  - Street side of the sidewalk
- Maintenance and repairs (you do it or you hire it done)
- Do the driving (order the Uber)
- Load the car
- Take out the trash
- Clean-up after the animals
- Share the housework
- Pay for dinner and drinks
- Support her show
- Move furniture
- Actual heavy lifting of every imaginable kind
- Heavy lifting also means making lots of money
- Heavy lifting includes continually but gently asserting your authority
- Do not be a *nice guy* (be good, kind, considerate, polite, and generous, but never be nice)[345]
- Spend lots of time with her

- Don't let her *go out on the town* (clubbing) without you
- Be the *man of the house*

"When I learned how to be a good man *rather than a* nice guy, *everything changed."*

~James Michael Sama

Chivalry

Modern chivalry is polite, honest, and kind behavior, especially by men toward women. Men behaving courteously toward women is considered chivalrous. Many women consider chivalry a lost art, while a strident few consider special courtesy extended to them as insulting and degrading.

---

[3] Women tend to be attracted to *bad boys, not* nice guys.

[4] "Nice guys finish last."

[5] "No more mister nice guy."

Of course, a modern woman speaks for herself and can independently take care of herself, but special courtesy could be considered romantic and affectionate.

Examples of chivalrous actions:

- Walking on the traffic side of sidewalks
- Standing when a woman arrives at a table
- Standing when a woman leaves a table
- Helping her with her coat
- Doing the driving
- Doing the paying
- Protecting her from embarrassment and humiliation
- Protecting her from insults and crime
- Polite manners and courtesy extended to her and others
- Good dining etiquette
- Dressing well to support her elegance
- Giving up your seat in crowded buses, lobbies, and waiting rooms.
- Holding open doors
- Pulling and placing chairs
- Noticing and remembering things of significance to her
- Sending unexpected flowers
- Offering your coat when she is cold
- Offering your arm, especially in treacherous terrain

- Preceding her down stairways and escalators
- Following her up stairways and escalators
- Practicing chivalry with your partner is similar to the coordination and collaboration of dancing. A man can look clumsy or foolish if the woman fails to accommodate his gestures. To avoid embarrassment, a graceful woman will anticipate chivalrous gestures. **For example:**
- Pause before doors
- Turn your body to allow access to your coat
- Pause to have your chair pulled
- Preceding men up stairways
- Pause to allow your man to proceed you down inclines and stairways

The Don'ts

Don'ts for men:

- Don't hold her purse
- Don't dress *metro*
- Don't listen to gossip and irrelevant bad news
- Don't let her *design* your spaces
- Don't *sell your motorcycle*
- Don't sell your bourbon collection

- Don't get rid of your porn collection
- Don't tell your friends you have to get her permission for anything
- Don't drive a *pussy vehicle*
- Don't let her dress you[6]
- Don't let her *emasculate* or *feminize* you
- Don't teach her anything[7] [8]
- Don't accept disrespect at home or in public (ironically, she will not respect you if you allow her to disrespect you)

---

[6] You are not a Ken doll.

Most men could use help with wardrobing, shoes, and personal style but not from your woman; go to a men's clothing store.

[7] Someone else must teach her; e.g. a ski instructor, golf instructor, et al.

[8] She does not like being subordinated to you for more than a few moments. She will disrespect you and be contrary and rebellious. She will respect an authoritative expert stranger and do everything he says without resistance.

- Don't undermine her show

Don'ts for women

- Don't let yourself be abused (physically, verbally, mentally)
- Don't let him disparage you in public
- Don't dress *sexy* to work
- Don't go *out* without him
- Don't feminize or emasculate your man
- Don't try to *dress* your man
- Don't instruct or mother your man.
- Don't raise your voice (disrespectful and a huge turn-off)

"I don't get enough credit in life for the things I manage not to say."
~Meg Rosoff

"If you say, "I'm just being honest," you are probably just being mean."
~Bert Wolfe

"Men don't like bossy women, period."
~Kevin Samuels, The Godfather

Stay Married

There Is tremendous power in staying married.

Having some rules for interactions can help keep couples glued together.

We are bound to argue, so let's explore methods of keeping it civil.

Some of us have traits that make relations more difficult.

Familiar Personality Traits that make arguments (heated discussions) more difficult:

- Argumentative
- Contrary
- Suspicious
- Untrusting
- Bossy (habits from work)
- Challenging
- Comparing
- Disagreeable
- Competitive
- Personalizing ("*You* always this and that.")
- Using your name in their rants
- Exaggerating (you always/everybody knows)
- Bringing up the past
- Shaming
- Blaming

- A need to be right
- Impatient

Rules of Engagement, AKA: Argument Rules:

- Don't personalize (leave *you* and *your* out of statements).
- Don't exaggerate (everybody knows that/you always).
- Don't make unfavorable personal comparisons ("You are just like your father").
- Don't generalize ("everybody knows that" or "people are saying").
- Don't impose taboos and constraints.
- Don't declare off-limits topics.
- Don't use emotional terrorism (crying, yelling, silence.)
- Don't commit psychological extortion (ultimatums, threats, consequences.)
- Don't make ultimatums.
- Don't argue when hungry and exhausted.
- Don't argue in the marital chambers.
- Don't vilify the other's gender ("That's all men think about," or "All you women are the same").
- Don't rehash the past.

Classic joke:

HOW TO MAKE A *MAN* HAPPY:

- Don't manage him too much.
- Sleep with him.
- Pretend you think he is cool.
- Don't bother him about his pastimes.

HOW TO MAKE A *WOMAN* HAPPY

It's not too difficult; a man needs to be:

1. Rich
2. Important
3. Charismatic
4. Influential
5. Her best friend
6. Her chief companion
7. Her lover
8. A brother
9. A father
10. A problem solver
11. A master
12. A chef
13. An electrician
14. A plumber
15. A mechanic
16. A carpenter

17. A decorator

18. A landscaper

19. A stylist

20. A sexologist

21. A gynecologist

22. A psychologist

23. Spiritual advisor

24. Her dedicated listener

25. Her bodyguard

26. A bellhop

27. A chauffeur

28. A heavy-lifter

29. A concierge

30. A luggage handler

31. An Uber driver

32. An escort

33. A pest exterminator

34. A healer

35. A good listener

36. An organizer

37. A logistician

38. A good father

39. A good pet parent

40. Neat and tidy

41. Well-groomed

42. Sympathetic

43. Physically fit

44. Athletic

45. Warm

46. Attentive

47. Gallant

48. A nice guy

49. Intelligent

50. Funny

51. Charming

52. Creative

53. Tender

54. Strong

55. Trustworthy

56. Loyal

57. Helpful

58. Friendly

59. Courteous

60. Kind

61. Obedient

62. Cheerful

63. Thrifty

64. Brave

65. Clean

66. Reverent

67. Understanding

68. Tolerant

69. Prudent

70. Ambitious

71. Generous

72. Charitable

73. Capable

74. Prepared

75. Determined

76. Enterprising

77. Dependable

78. Romantic

79. Passionate

WITHOUT FORGETTING TO:

1. Give her compliments regularly

2. Go shopping with her

3. Hold her purse

4. Be honest

5. Be rich

6. Never stress her out

7. Never look at other girls

AND AT THE SAME TIME:

1. Give her lots of attention
2. Listen to her a lot
3. Give her lots of time, especially time for herself
4. Give her lots of space.
5. Never worry about where she goes.

MOST OF ALL:

Never forget:

1. Birthdays
2. Anniversaries
3. Valentine's Day
4. Arrangements she makes

See, what's so hard about that? Can't we all just get along?

Jokes aside, work it out and stay married.

Maybe I should rephrase my basic premise:

From:

"Who you choose to marry is the most important financial decision you will ever make."

To:

"Who you <u>choose to stay married to</u> is the most important decision you will ever make."

Marriage vs. Wedding

Women, in particular, need to be careful not to have an active but hidden childhood goal to have a wonderful wedding while essentially forgetting the fundamental purpose of getting married for life.

"As a wedding minister, I have witnessed couples focusing all their attention on pulling off an amazing wedding while essentially forgetting their fundamental purpose of successfully getting married for life."

~Bert Wolfe

The Honeymoon and Other Romantic Touchstones

Romantic touchstones are essential foundations for a long-lasting relationship. Your relationship is built on the foundations of unforgettable key events. When shit hits the fan like it will, you will fall back on and rely on your romantic touchstones.

- ♥ First introduction
- ♥ The first date
- ♥ The first kiss
- ♥ The third date
- ♥ The proposal
- ♥ The ring
- ♥ The wedding
- ♥ The honeymoon
- ♥ First anniversary
- ♥ Sunday drives
- ♥ Romantic personal rituals

Don't skip or short-shrift any of these events; you will need your underpinnings.

Romantic Habits

Romantic habits and rituals are in this category. Using romantic habits as touchstones, you can keep things together when things get seriously rough.

Rituals:

- ♥ Holding hands in public
- ♥ Holding hands while walking
- ♥ Holding hands before sleep

- ♥ Greeting upon waking
- ♥ Kissing at stair landings
- ♥ Pet names
- ♥ Private references
- ♥ Shared adventures
- ♥ Shared stories
- ♥ Code words
- ♥ Providing all kinds of chivalry
- ♥ Accepting all kinds of chivalry

Conclusion: Once you are married, stay married. Work that shit out.

Marriage is not an experiment; it is a lifetime commitment.

If you don't see it that way, don't get married.

Chapter 5 Children

"Unless you are truly rich, raising children will be, far and away, the most expensive thing you will do in your life."

~Bert Wolfe

From a financial planning perspective, spouses and children are pure liabilities. Therefore, think of children as expensive luxuries. Technically speaking, spouses and children are no longer economic necessities (assets.)

~Bert Wolfe

If you feel a need to indulge in procreation, you had better prepare yourself financially. Children will cost their parents one million dollars each. To be a responsible parent, you must be a significant earner.

~Bert Wolfe

Odds are, you will have children. Procreation and raising offspring approximate life's greater purpose. Therefore, childraising is an enormously essential commitment.

Our animal bodies are hardwired to procreate, and the biological imperative to propagate the species is compelling.

A conscious human needs to take careful control of this function.

As profoundly meaningful as procreation and child-rearing can be, it can easily be a financial and psychological disaster.

Decades ago, in more rural conditions, children could be assets. Children could contribute to farm chores or work in the family business. In the past, children could work for money to help support the family; this is no longer the case.

Children are no longer financial assets in today's world. Frankly, children have become liabilities. Children are nothing more than a costly, time-consuming hobby and one of the most expensive hobbies a couple could ever share.

Think it through.

Ask yourself questions like these:

- Why have children?
- How many children?
- What do the children get?
- What do you get out of making children?
- What do you get out of raising children?
- What do you get from raising someone else's children?

- How long do they stay? How long will each child be with you?
- What is the required age of departure? 18/21/30?
- Will they be allowed to return? Boomerang?
- Room and board for life?
- How long do you support your children?

- Will you pay for college?
- What kind of college?
- In-state or out?
- How many years?
- What kind of degree?
- What if a child has special needs?
- You may need to support a child financially for your entire life.
- This is a real possibility.
- It happens plenty often enough.
- Can you handle this kind of burden for the rest of your life?

I am not against children. I am against having children live a sub-par upbringing.

I hate to see people procreating who cannot afford to do it well.

If you choose to procreate, how many years do you plan to afford (pay for) each kid?

Room and Board

- Room and board for life? Only if:
- o You are truly rich
- o Your child is disabled
- o You are codependent
- o You are a sucker/chump
- How long do you plan to support your children financially?
- o If your children are mostly mentally and physically able, you would be wise to set and announce the *dates of separation* from your financial support.
- o Can you insist on their financial independence and self-sufficiency?
- o Do you have the emotional strength to stop supporting your grown children?
- o Can you sustain your position of emancipation?

Typical Reasons Given for Having Children:

- To see what they will look like.
- We can create something together.
- Enjoyment and fun.
- To be good parents.
- To contribute something to the world.
- It's what everybody does.
- You feel compelled to have them.
- The church expects us to.
- My parents want grandkids.
- They will take care of me when I am old.

Let's face it; the typical reasons tend to look selfish, naïve, and poorly considered. These reasons for having kids have nothing to do with the happiness and success of the child.

Let's examine these logics:

- **To see what they will look like.** Narcissistic – how is this good for anybody?
- **We can create something together.** Children will be an expensive, stressful, time-consuming responsibility – how about you create a garden together or create a charity or a business?
- **Enjoyment and fun.** Sometimes children will be fun, but predominantly, children will be an enormous responsibility – the source of tremendous hard work, stress, and anxiety.

- **To be a good parent.** What does being a good parent do for you? Bragging rights? Showing off? What is a good parent anyway compared to what, a bad parent?

- **To contribute something to the world.** Like what? Isn't the world already straining with overpopulation and environmental overload? How will making more children help? Will your children be astonishing geniuses who save the world somehow?

- **It's what everybody does.** That sounds like a good reason not to do it.

- **You feel compelled to have them.** What is the source of that compulsion? Is this your need? Or some built-in cellular or genetic drive to propagate the species?

- **The church expects us to.** Who is the boss of you? What does the church get out of that? (More parishioners and more tithing?)

- **My parents want grandkids.** Are you sure they do? Do they want the trouble and expense of raising another set of children? Are you obligated to provide grandchildren?

- **They will take care of me when I am old.** If you need someone to care for you when you get old, you will have failed financially and health-wise. Do you plan to burden your children with your failing health and finances?

Anti-kid?

Prompting these questions may seem *anti-kid*. Not at all. This author generally loves kids. But I don't love the idea of senseless, thoughtless procreation.

Here are some questions to prompt people to think more deeply. Using an earnest tone, ask: "Don't you just love children?" Typically, I get a gushingly positive response that they love kids. Then I ask if they like bratty, ill-behaved kids who have no manners and appear to be budding young sociopaths. The truth is that we do enjoy *some* kids, but certainly not *all* kids. We enjoy well-mannered, polite children who seem free of evil intentions, and we do not enjoy ill-mannered prospective criminals who swing cats around by the tail.

The same goes for *old people*. "Don't you just love old people?" Not necessarily. We like sweet, honest older people who share wisdom and good stories, and we dislike mean people who have simply grown old. Criminals and perverts get old, too, so no, we don't like *all* old people any more than we like *all* children.

Food for thought.

"It is wrong to bear children out of need, wrong to use a child to alleviate loneliness, wrong to provide purpose in life by reproducing another copy of oneself. It is wrong also to seek immortality by spewing one's germ into the future as though sperm contains your consciousness!"

~ Irvin D. Yalom

It seems that allowing children more time to mature gradually has its benefits. However, there is some danger that a sheltered child will find it difficult to cope when presented with adult situations.

"Delaying exposure to alcohol, then, could make young adults less prepared to deal with drinking in college."

~Jean Twenge,

Professor of Psychology, San Diego State University

Get a Job

It might be wise to require your children to have jobs. Do your children a lifetime favor by requiring them to have jobs in high school.

Benefits of a teen job:

- Learn to show up
- Learn to be punctual
- Learn to interact with all ages of work peers
- Learn good work habits
- Learn a personal work ethic
- Learn to communicate on a professional level
- Learn decision-making
- Learn how to make their own money
- See how much the government takes
- Experience of spending hard-earned money
- Discover the ratio of low pay/expensive life

"The same might be true of teens who don't work, drive, or go out much in high school. Yes, they are less likely to have an accident, but they may arrive at college or the workplace less prepared to make decisions on their own."

~Jean Twenge,

Professor of Psychology, San Diego State University

In today's world, slower childhood development may be a good way to mature into adulthood, but certainly, by age 25, any young person should be up to speed building an independent life.

"For parents, this might mean making a concerted effort to push your teenagers out of the house more. Otherwise, they might want to live with you forever."

~Jean Twenge,

Professor of Psychology, San Diego State University

There are three classic old-school options for offspring at age 18. The young adult must choose one of three options or permanently move out.

- Military
- College
- A full-time job paying rent to parents.

There is no *board* in these three options – only *room*.

"In my day, parents 'sawed the 18-year-old's corner off the dinner table' – so there was nothing to return to."

~Jerry C. – father of three

"I explain to my patients that abused children often find it hard to disentangle themselves from their dysfunctional families, whereas children grow away from good, loving parents with far less conflict. After all, isn't that the task of a good parent, to enable the child to leave home?"

~ Irvin Yalom, Psychotherapist

"It's not an empty nest until they get their crap out of the basement."

~Unknown

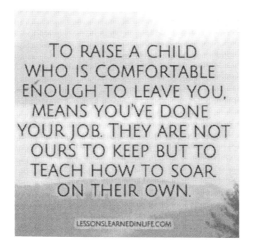

TO RAISE A CHILD WHO IS COMFORTABLE ENOUGH TO LEAVE YOU, MEANS YOU'VE DONE YOUR JOB. THEY ARE NOT OURS TO KEEP BUT TO TEACH HOW TO SOAR ON THEIR OWN.

LESSONSLEARNEDINLIFE.COM

Child Support

The term *child support* is typically used in the context of an absentee parent. Official Child Support is court-ordered. Court-ordered child support is much less than an onboard parent's spending; all the incidental expenses add up to much more than mere child support.

An *onboard* parent won't think of themselves as paying child support because it is embedded in their overall household living expenses.

Figure that child support will last thirty years for each child, so realistically, figure on at least 35 years of total child support for two or three overlapping children.

When Do Children Come of Age?

13) Teen years begin

14) Right to work part-time

15) Learner's permit

16) Right to work fulltime

16) Age of sexual consent

16) Driver's license

18) Right to vote

18) Right to serve in the military

18) Right to own firearms

20) No longer a teenager

21) Right to drink alcohol

25) Off the parent's dole?

25–35) Typical age range of bong-smoking gamers who squat in their parent's basement.

Allowances

Will you still give your children an *allowance* or *spending money* after the age of 18? When do you expect them to fend for themselves? How will you foster their work ethic?

My best suggestion is that at the age of 18, all *allowances* end. In the United States, childhood ends at the age of 18. 18-year-olds can vote and go to war. War is bad business for everybody, but we don't send children to fight in wars. When a person turns 20, you can't even call them a teenager anymore; let's just say they are adults. Oddly, adults are not allowed to drink alcohol until they are 21. Indeed, at the age of 21, when full adulthood is granted, it is hard for me to understand why a parent would be underwriting their offspring's finances. Why would an adult be getting money from their parents? How did that offspring fail to become a gainfully employed adult? Did they fail to get a useful education? Are they mentally or emotionally disabled? Are they pathologically lazy?

I don't know the answers, but these are questions worth asking; it is so widespread that young adults are substantially supported for years by very hard-working parents.

If you happen to be seriously rich, well then, maybe all bets are off; support your adult children for as long as you want. However, I wonder if that is helping them become mature, contributing members of society.

Suppose you are a wealthy parent who wants to share *the wealth* with your offspring. In that case, I suggest you demand they earn their own money before you match their pay dollar-for-dollar. That way, they can be a member of a wealthy family that expects everyone in the family to shoulder responsibility, work, contribute something, and earn money.

"Marry before you carry."

~Kevin Samuels

Planned Parenthood:

- When do you want children?
- Should you be married first?
- How many children do you want?
- Seriously, why that many?
- Are you a *breeder*?
- What is your logic?
- How will you support those lives?
- Can you afford children?
- Do you know how to parent?

Procreation is entirely different from *parenting*. It is one thing to have sex and make a baby; it is quite another to raise that child for 30 years.

If you have a plan and truly believe procreation is the right thing to do, then more power to you.

Unplanned Parenthood

"Having an unplanned child may be the single most catastrophic financial mistake a person could ever make."

~Bert Wolfe

An unplanned child may be the single most catastrophic financial mistake a person could ever make, much worse than the expense of a divorce.

A failed marriage could cost you half of everything plus seven years of alimony. But, having an unplanned or even unwanted child will cost you at least 18 years of child support, and just one child will be fantastically more expensive than a divorce. Unless you are seriously rich, breeding mistakes are catastrophically more expensive than marital mistakes. There are two financial considerations here: 1) total expense and 2) term of time.

The financial obligation lasts more than ten years longer than alimony. A typical failed marriage with two kids produces a nearly impossible financial burden. If you provide for three children two years apart, that will be $20 + 2 + 2 = 24$ years of financial support. The commitment could run close to thirty years if you can't launch them. Thirty-year-old kids living in their parents' basements are all too common. Thirty years is the span of an entire career!

Then there will be grandchildren. It would be typical to end up with five or more grandchildren. Let's face it; you will not disavow or neglect your grandchildren. You will spend significant time and money on your grandkids. You will end up babysitting and petsitting.

You only get grandchildren by having your own kids first.

Note that *providing* for children is not the same as *raising* children. The time and devotion required to raise children is immense.

An unplanned child is a catastrophic setback to a life plan.

An unplanned child could lead to an unplanned marriage.

An unplanned child within a marriage will create marital strain. An unplanned child could break a marriage.

Take direct personal control of birth control. Do not leave control of the most critical consequence of your entire life in someone else's hands.

Procreation and marriage need to be well-planned.

What kind of education will you afford your children?
- Preschool?
- Home school?
- Tutoring?
- Private school?
- Charter school?
- Public school?
- Government indoctrination center?
- Community college?
- State college?
- Trade school?
- University?
- Ivy league?

Sincerely ask yourself if procreation is worth it. Sincerely ask yourself if you can afford it. The chart below illustrates the catastrophic financial setback of fouled-up procreation and failed marriages.

Failed Marriage with Two Children

Middle-Class	Upper Middle	Affluent
Half of everything at the time of separation:		
$200,000	$500,000	$1,050,000
Child expense for 25 years:		
$500,000	$1,000,000	$2,500,000
Second child:		
$500,000	$1,000,000	$2,500,000

Total failed Marriage Financial Penalty:

$1,200,000.00	$2,5000,00.00	**$6,050,000**

Two children: Two million dollars divided by twenty-five years = eighty thousand dollars a year.

Think I am exaggerating? Okay, reduce my figures by half: One million dollars divided by twenty-five years = forty thousand dollars a year.

Maybe the spouse pays half: twenty thousand dollars a year. It will be more than that in any scenario.

The High Likelihood of Additional Children Due to Remarriage.

There is a high likelihood of additional children due to remarriage. After a divorce, you will be dating during middle age; therefore, your prospective mates will already have children of their own – as do you. Combining the children of two families plus any new, additional offspring, you could have 5 or 6 children after repeated marriages.

Costs of Kids:

- Daycare
- Commuting so kids have better schools and life
- Food
- Lodging
- Clothing
- Toys
- School supplies
- Travel expenses
- Healthcare
- Babysitting
- Sports
- Private school
- Classes
- Lessons

- Tutoring
- Stay-at-home parent
- Summer camps
- School trips
- Healthcare
- Special needs
- Special interests: music, horses, arts, martial arts, special skills, etc.
- Pets
- Veterinarian expenses
- Travel and lodging for sports/performances/competitions
- Automobile, plus expenses
- Auto insurance
- Legal trouble
- Tuition
- Books
- Lab and class supplies
- Travel
- College room and board
- Competitive vacations (between exes)
- Bar mitzvahs
- Weddings
- Grandkids

Most people earn for about forty years. Wages minus taxes minus two kids minus lifestyle minus everything else; what will be left?

Most people do all of these things:

- Nonoptimum marriage
- Divorce
- Untargeted education
- Random procreation
- Non-lineal career development
- Competitive, materialistic spending
- Expensive dwelling
- Expensive furniture and decor
- Expensive automobiles
- Sleep deprivation
- Debt assumption
- Expensive vacations
- Long commutes
- Remarriage
- More children

What if a person chose not to follow that pattern? What could their lifestyle and finances look like?

Most Significant Expenses of Life:

- Under-productive marriage

- Children
- Divorce
- Unfocused college *education.*
- Bad luck
- Healthcare problems
- Retirement

Things we don't consider when we are young:

- How many years will I work?
- Will I marry?
- Will I have children?
- Will I be able to afford my dreams?

Men

Enough Children - The Big V

When is enough enough? How long will you wait to make yourself financially safe from unplanned child expenses? How long will you risk it?!

A middle-class child will cost $50 K a year for twenty years. That's a million dollars. A vasectomy might cost you $2,500, while a child will cost you a million dollars; you do the math.

For god's sake, when you are clearly finished procreating, immediately get a vasectomy.

Some men worry that a vasectomy will somehow diminish the enjoyment of sex. There is no biological basis for this.

The opposite is true. When the couple no longer has any worry or concern about pregnancy, the sex is less stressed and more relaxed – carefree, if you will.

Getting a vasectomy may create an incredible sense of relief. It's so worth it.

So just do it.

Get the Big V.

Get 'er done.

How Strong is your urge to have children? And why?

What are the sources of the urge to have children?

- Social indoctrination?
- Societal pressure?
- Religious imperative?
- Parental expectation?
- Sibling encouragement?
- Biological/Cellular program?
- DNA coding?
- Genetic imperative?
- Peer group pressure?
- Mental Implants?

"To build children, you must first be built yourself. Otherwise, you'll seek children out of animal needs or loneliness or to patch the holes in yourself. Your task as a parent is to produce not another self, another Josef, but something higher. It's to produce a creator."

~ Irvin D. Yalom,

When Nietzsche Wept: A Novel of Obsession

Procreation

How to get it right, or at least lower the odds of failure:

- Don't make babies until married for at least five years.

- Don't get married before the age of thirty. Then, give the marriage at least five years to become established and stable. You owe this to yourselves and the children. Don't be selfishly eager to make babies.

- Therefore, you should not make babies until you are at least 35.

- A 35-year-old would presumably be more emotionally and financially capable of making wise decisions about having children and how they will be raised.

- However, after 35, pregnancy is statistically riskier.

Waiting sounds like logical advice, but here is the rub. *Advanced maternal age* describes a pregnancy where the mother is over 35, and a mother over 35 is at more risk for miscarriage, congenital disorders, and high blood pressure. In the past, the term was *geriatric pregnancy*. There is no universal definition, but typically, it is considered a pregnancy over age 35.

Q: I'm finally well remarried but have alimony and three kids. What do I do now?

A: Frankly, the damage is done for most people in your situation. You may be hosed as far as achieving financial freedom. If you want to be an exception, my powerfully simplistic answer is that you must now *out-create* the situation you have let yourself into. You must radically change your habitual operating patterns to overcome such an extreme financial burden.

If you have a good spouse, marriage, and kids, enjoy and love them, and give your kids each a copy of this book so they can start their lives with their eyes wide open.

Surveys Say

If you conduct an informal survey of older, experienced people, you may be surprised at the perspective they have gained from living a long time.

Getting older people to tell you their authentic truths takes some doing.

Most people are uncomfortable accepting or acknowledging that they have made fundamental mistakes. People want to feel like they mostly did things right and will typically say they wouldn't change much of what they did. However, we want the experienced older person to disclose what they did wrong and right.

If you want a true perspective from a well-experienced person, you need to frame the questions so they don't have to expose that they made serious life choice mistakes. People will often tell you that it never occurred to them that they even had life choices. For example, societal and biological programming urges us to marry as soon as possible and start making a family of children, and pretty much everyone does this.

So, you frame the questions as theoretical alternatives for past choices.

If you ask a person if they regret having children, they will predictably respond with something like this: "Of course not; having children was the most important thing I ever did."

"I love my children."

Of course, they do.

If you ask them if they had a chance to do things over, would they still have chosen to have children? They still might feel compelled to claim that it was worth it to have had children.

I have found that if you get a person into a conversation they feel safe in and you ask questions more neutrally, experienced people will consistently tell you that, yes, they did marry too young, and, yes, they started having children too soon.

Most honest people will acknowledge that they would have had a better life if they had married later and started having children later.

They will acknowledge that they would be much better off if they had married later in life and had fewer children. Their marriage would be stronger and more enjoyable. Their children would be happier and more balanced. And their finances would be stronger. In short, they would have a higher quality of life.

From a financial planning perspective, spouses and children are pure liabilities. Therefore, think of children as expensive luxuries. Technically speaking, spouses and children are no longer economic necessities (assets.)

If you feel a need to indulge in procreation, you had better prepare yourself financially. Children will cost their parents one million dollars each. To be a responsible parent, you must be a <u>significant</u> earner.

Here are some socially unacceptable questions:

- "What if you purposely never got married?"
- "What if you married only for strategic purposes?"
- "What if you never produced any children?"
- "If you got a chance to do it all over, would you get more formal education?" The answer is invariably a yes.
- "If you could change the past, would you want to commute less?" Overwhelming yes!
- "Is the scramble to *keep up with the Joneses* worth it?" Resounding no.
- "Would you like to have traveled more?" Universal yes.
- "Would you like to have gotten more sleep?" Duh.
- "Would you like to have spent more time on hobbies and personal interests?" Of course.

Ask an older person: "If you had not had children, how would your life be different today?"

The oldster may confess they would be healthier and more prosperous without children. And that they would have seen more of the world and would have had more adventures. Marrying and having children seems to be biological, social, and religious imperatives. Marriage and children are tremendous life-consuming responsibilities. To accomplish anything more than simply raising a well-balanced family is barely practical. Raising that family is the only important thing you may accomplish with your life. Realistically, too few resources of time, money, and personal energy will be available for more than raising your family. Raising a family is all-consuming.

And then, if the marriage and family don't work out, you will try to start another one; you will use up your life in that pursuit. It may be worth the endeavor, and maybe not.

It might be wise to consider all of this while still young and not committed.

If you fail to have children, you will be considered odd and even a heretic.

My simple questions to you:

- Is it truly *your* imperative to marry and procreate?
- Is it really your idea?
- If it is, what is your detailed financial plan to support your imperative?

"Procreation is never accidental. Pregnancy may be poorly planned, but it is never accidental. Various 'before, during, and after' forms of birth control make it technically and scientifically impossible to bear a child accidentally."

~Bert Wolfe

Procreation is Optional

You are not required to procreate, and procreation is never accidental. Pregnancy may be poorly planned, but it is never accidental. Various *before, during, and after* forms of birth control make it technically and scientifically impossible to bear a child *accidentally*. There are over forty forms of birth control and even an implant that prevents pregnancy for up to five years. Why do so many women reach for abortions?

Abortion

What is late-term abortion to you:

- Irresponsible behavior?
- Poor planning?
- Birth control?
- Freedom of choice?
- Problem-solving?
- Elective surgery?
- Healthcare alternative?
- An unfortunate necessity?
- Termination?
- Killing?
- Murder?

Abortion is the last-ditch method of preventing procreation. It is extremely rare for all other forms of birth control to fail. At any level, given any moral consideration, abortion is a terrible alternative. Abortion may be murder. I don't believe so, but the grizzly details of late-term abortions make me think it might be. I believe that women should have the right to abortion. However, regardless of ethics and morality, abortion is a risky surgical procedure. At the very least, abortions send women on a rollercoaster ride of strong hormonal effects. The mental, emotional, and physiological effects of having an abortion can be extreme—avoid abortions at all costs.

Forty percent of women who have had abortions have had two or more. Using abortion as a form of routine birth control is unconscionable.

Childlessness

Advantages of having no children:
- Nicer things
- More sleep
- More sex
- Less stress
- Better health
- Better vacations
- More orderly household
- Simpler family logistics
- More money

- More adult types of fun
- Better adult types of activities
- Better intellectual pursuits
- Massively more personal time
- Fewer worries

Advantages of Having Children:

- The joy of raising them?
- The special love of your own child?
- The love and appreciation they will return to you?
- Companionship?
- Entertainment?

Getting married and having kids had better be worth it because the costs of money, time, and personal sacrifice are genuinely tremendous.

Winter is Coming

Breeding Time Line:

Women need to finish procreating by age 35 to avoid the dangers of geriatric pregnancy. This means marrying before 30.

The "Danger Zone" starts for women at age 40. Beyond the age of forty, women are unlikely to marry.

How many hours does a parent's workday require?

8 - sleep.

1 - waking up, personal body care, getting dressed.

1.5 - getting children up, fed, and delivered to their school with lunch and books.

2 - commuting to and from work.

9 - work.

3 - meals: breakfast .5, lunch 1, Dinner 1.5 – plus procurement, prep, and clean-up.

2 - household maintenance, cleaning, laundry, yard, and repairs.

1 - errands.

1.5 - exercise.

1 - personal wind-down at home.

1 - management of children: love, affection, attention, homework, discipline.

1 - pet care.

1 - family time.

1 - spouse time.

Thirty-four total hours out of 24 – oops!

10 hours over.

Try shaving this down. You need to cut 10 hours out of your day.

Sure, a husband and wife will try to share the burdens; nevertheless, you have a severe time deficit. Maybe the parents share duties and shave off two whole hours. Now, you still have eight negative hours to shave. Okay, you reduce your sleep to 5 hours, and now you still have 5 hours to cut. You cut all household duties, yet 3 hours remain to cut.

You cannot get more than 24 hours, so something always must give. Essential responsibilities will be shorted: work, sleep, the children, and a little of everything.

Extra Time Demands:

- What if your boss demands overtime?
- What if your commute is more than two hours a day?
- What if one of the parents gets sick?
- What if a child must stay home due to illness?
- How will you attend your children's activities?
- What about your sports and hobbies?
- How will you have a personal life?
- Where is the *me time*?

These are tough questions with non-optimum answers.

3 stupid stages of life!

Teen age:
Have Time + Energy ...but No Money

Working Age:
Have Money + Energy ...but No Time

Old age:
Have Time + Money ...but no Energy

"Marry Before You Carry"

~Kevin Samuels

The Godfather

Optimum Sequence

All evidence indicates that the most optimum sequence looks like this:

1. Career training and education
2. Career initiation
3. Career development
4. Dating
5. Marriage
6. Financial footing
7. Children

Violating this sequence won't necessarily ruin your life, but staying on a sound financial track will require extra effort and creativity.

Ex-nuptial Child: a child born outside of marriage.

- Whose last name will the child be given?
- Will the child have a father figure?
- Will the child be sufficiently financially supported?
- Will the child experience a complete, wholesome family life?
- Will the child have one parent or two?

Does Society Need Your Children?

Should you have children? I don't know. I am just asking you to think about it first.

Will society benefit from you having children? I don't know.

Two men I admire, Elon Musk and Jordon Peterson, emphatically posit that we need more people on Earth. I am confused by this.

I experience life from the idea that our infrastructures are overwhelmed by too many people.

Resources always seem to be in short supply. Demand appears to outstrip supply in most categories. Too many people need more than we can supply. Pollution, poverty, and hunger are everywhere. To me, it looks like we have too many mouths to feed. Since college, I have advocated for *Zero Population Growth*. Maybe I am wrong.

I remain adamant that thoughtless procreation leads to relative poverty.

Maybe the world needs more people, but populating the planet is not my job.

"Procreation is entirely different from parenting. It is one thing to have sex and make a baby; It is quite another to raise that child for 30 years."

~**Bert Wolfe**

Parenting

Do you know how to raise a child successfully? Who taught you? What qualifies you to be a good parent? Do you have the time and money to raise children?

To what degree do you plan to delegate your child-rearing:

- Nanny?
- Au pair?
- Preschool?
- Public school?
- Private school?
- Boarding school?

- Tutors?
- Your parents?
- Stay-at-home parent?
- Homeschooling?
- Work-study?
- Travel study?

Chapter questions:

- Will you have children?
- To what degree will you raise your children yourself?
- How will having children contribute to the extraordinary life of your dreams?

Conclusion: Plan, in detail, the total expense of each child before you commit yourself to that time-consuming monetary responsibility. If you can't afford them, don't make them. Think, plan, and marry before you breed.

Chapter 6 Family

"You go through life wondering what is it all about, but at the end of the day, it's all about family."

~Rod Stewart

"I sustain myself with the love of family."

~Maya Angelou

"In every conceivable manner, the family is a link to our past, bridge to our future."

~Alex Haley

Am I disqualified from enjoying a family experience?

What ifs:

- What if I don't have kids of my own?
- What if I have no genetic family?
- What if I am estranged from my genetic family?
- What if I am still single?
- What if I am divorced?
- What if I followed my career and now live far from my birth family?

- What if I am estranged from my birth family?
- What if I am an orphan?
- What if I am an only child?

We need to define the concept of family to suit our situations. We need to form our own family units. Outside of our birth family, we can decide who we want in whatever grouping we think of as family. People need their own tribe for safety, comfort, and survival.

Declining Birth Rates

Declining first-world birthrates are undermining the traditional model of an extended large family.

Prominent sociologists have suggested that the First World is experiencing an accelerating birth rate decline.

"Virtually every developed country is below two, and it's been that way for 20 or 30 years. Yes, in some countries, their population is declining, but for the world, that's just not the case."

~Joseph Chamie, Demographer

Elon Musk tweeted, not for the first time, that "population collapse due to low birth rates is a much bigger risk to civilization than global warming."

This author believes the world is straining with overpopulation and environmental overload.

The lower economic strata are growing. The number of people depending on the government is ever-increasing. Goods and services are scarce and expensive because too many people need them. The natural environment is contaminated and under strain to sustain itself because too many people are trampling it. We are building houses on fruitful agricultural land. Housing is constantly in short supply.

Churches, big corporations, and the government encourage population growth to produce more contributing tithers, paying customers, and taxpayers.

Meanwhile, the dependent classes are burgeoning. In contrast, the willing working class is shrinking. Taxes are becoming so high they appear to be approaching breaking-point levels.

"As the population ages and birth rates decline in some areas of the globe, that could put strain on social systems."

~ **Jen Christensen**

"I don't think in the US it's an issue of collapse because we can certainly open the faucet for more immigrants anytime we want to. We'll have no paucity of people who want to come through the door to immigrate here in the future. Immigrants and their children are younger than the population as a whole, and so that will help to keep the population from aging as well."

~William Frey, Demographer

We each define and create our own version of family. People often ask, "What is the purpose of life?" A plausible answer is that the purpose of life is to serve relationships and family. The traditional concept of family may be changing. Nevertheless, the need for family is built into our DNA. The need for family is fundamental to our survival and future security. For most individuals, some form of family is essential to thier peace of mind, sense of future, and sense of security.

When your working life is over, who will your people be? Keep your chosen family in mind as you progress your life.

"The essential value of family is loyalty."
~Bert Wolfe

"The strength of a family, like the strength of an army, is in its loyalty to each other."

~Mario Puzo

"Call it a clan, call it a network, call it a tribe, call it a family: Whatever you call it, whoever you are, you need one."

~Jane Howard

Chapter questions:

1. What is your definition of family?
2. Can you be loyal to your family?
3. Is your family loyal to you?

Conclusion: In one way or another, a family may be the most important asset you can create and build for yourself. Whether you have a genetic or chosen family, family is your foundation for long-term success. Do not neglect your family while you are busy building a career and a lifestyle. When shit hits the fan, it is family you will turn to, and it is family that will put you back on your feet.

Chapter 7 Education and Training

"I came into the world with two priceless advantages: good health and a love of learning. When I left school at the age of fifteen, I was halfway through the tenth grade. I left for two reasons, economic necessity being the first of them. More important was that school was interfering with my education."

~ Louis L'Amour
Education of a Wandering Man

"Both animals and humans can be successfully trained; only humans can be educated."

~Bert Wolfe

Differences between Humans and Animals

- We take longer to become adults.
- We go to school – sometimes for a long time.
- We have voluntary birth control.
- We live longer than most animals.
- We are sentient (aware of being aware.)

- We use tools extensively.

- We have language – spoken and written.

- We have books.

- We have music.

- We record history.

- We have computers and machines.

- We build infrastructure.

- We adapt to environments by using technology.

- We have a monetary exchange.

- We have encoded laws – and enforcement.

- We have codes of conduct and honor.

- We accessorize!

Take advantage of being human; get yourself well-educated. Devote yourself to *lifelong learning*.

Learning the *Hard Way*

We undoubtedly learn better when we learn the hard way. The *hard way* would be learning all by yourself – making classic mistakes and suffering the consequences of them without help or guidance from others. These lessons embed themselves more firmly into our memories and consciousness.

Learning the hard way is good and bad. While learning the hard way may embed itself more strongly, it takes tremendous time and energy and can be psychologically hindering. I've seen the *hard way* learners get exhausted and psyched out enough to abandon their goals and settle for mediocre results.

We don't have time to learn everything the hard way; we must learn from others and save ourselves from the wasted time and agony of learning everything the hard way.

"Most people waste too much time learning from their own mistakes. We do not need to learn and discover everything on our own, and we do not need to build our life skills exclusively with our own painful errors."
~**Bert Wolfe**

"The capacity to learn is a gift; The ability to learn is a skill; The willingness to learn is a choice."
~ **Brian Herbert, House Harkonnen**

There are many sources of wisdom and knowledge:

- Teachers
- Mentors
- Councilors
- Guides
- Instructors
- Gurus
- Schools
- Libraries
- Books
- Videos
- Apprenticeships
- Training
- Instruction
- Studying
- The internet
- Siri
- Youtube

"No matter how much I admire our schools, I know that no university exists that can provide an education; what a university can provide is an outline to give the learner a direction and guidance. The rest one has to do for oneself."

~ Louis L'Amour, Education of a Wandering Man

"No one can 'get' an education; for of necessity, education is a continuing process. If it does nothing else, it should provide students with the tools for learning, acquaint them with methods of study and research, methods of pursuing an idea. We can only hope they come upon an idea they wish to pursue."

~ Louis L'Amour, Education of a Wandering Man

"The saving grace and secret weapon for all of us with average IQs is education - and lots of it. I mean formal education, but I especially mean self-education."

~Bert Wolfe

Learning, Training, and Education

Only the truly rich can afford the classic, mostly useless, *liberal arts* college education that the middle class is so fond of. The irony is that the truly rich more typically focus on business and law degrees because they will inherit serious wealth management responsibilities.

You can take an interest in art history and French literature after securing your fortune.

Is College for You?

- Skip college and go straight to working?
- Forget college and go to trade school?
- Attend some college after high school?
- Attend local college while still in High School?
- Go to a trade school?
- Graduate college with a frivolous degree?
- Graduate college with a useful degree?
- Take a break and return to college?
- Start or finish college later in life?

"If your degree has the word Studies at the end of it, you will probably be poor. If you have a degree in art or philosophy, you will likely have serious trouble just paying off your student loans, much less making a decent living."

~Bert Wolfe

We all know which degrees lead to financial success and which degrees lead to the doldrums.

Overlooked Educational Subjects:

(Skills and Training that you *should* have that most people don't)

- Advanced First Aid or better
- AED proficiency (Automated External Defibrillator)
- CPR proficiency (Cardio Pulmonary Resuscitation)
- Power Tool Safety Knowledge
- Household Safety
- Fire Safety
- High-speed Collision Avoidance Training
- Automobile Maintenance
- Home Owner Maintenance
- Health and personal well-being
- Nutrition
- Gardening
- Farming
- Financial management
- Financial planning
- Basics of the legal system
- Parenting classes
- Marital counseling
- Personal safety training
- Self-defense
- Firearms proficiency and safety

- Addiction and codependency
- Map and compass navigation
- Outdoor Survival
- Disaster preparedness

Self-Education

Recommended reading: **Education of a Wandering Man** by Louis L'Amour

"Education is everywhere, prompting one to think, to consider, to remember."

Louis L'Amour,

Education of a Wandering Man

"A book is less important for what it says than for what it makes you think."

~ Louis L'Amour, Education of a Wandering Man

"No matter how much I admire our schools, I know that no university exists that can provide an education; what a university can provide is an outline to give the learner a direction and guidance. The rest one has to do for oneself."

~ Louis L'Amour, Education of a Wandering Man

Notes:

You will earn far more $ with a targeted graduate degree.

Chapter questions:

- What is your educational strategy?
- What is your cost-benefit analysis for your education?

-

Conclusion: Will your education leverage your money-making career and lifestyle enough to provide an extra-ordinary life?

Dedicate yourself to *life-long learning.*

Chapter 8 Your Career

What You Do for Money

"Most Americans are heavily indebted tax paying wage slaves."

~Bert Wolfe

If you want to avoid the endless, lifelong grind of making barely enough to eat, sleep, and pay taxes, you must strategically consider your education and career path.

What is the difference between a career and just a job?

A *career* is a trained occupation or profession committed to a significant period of a person's life and with opportunities for leadership, progress, and fulfillment. A career is an undertaking that feels like *making a difference*, like a person's lifework. A *job* is more like an hourly wage position. People work jobs to earn money to pay the bills. What feeling do you want from your livelihood?

What kind of satisfaction?

Making Money by What Activity?

- Job?
- Vocation?

- Occupation?
- Business?
- Calling?
- Employment?
- Career?
- Line of Work?
- Line?
- Profession?
- Passion?

What qualities does the job have?

- Tasks?
- Chores?
- Obligations?
- Engagements?
- Projects?
- Assignments?
- Errands?
- Positions?
- Situations?
- Employment?
- Jobs?
- Conscription?

- Work?
- Production?
- Duty?
- Responsibility?
- Penance?
- Fulfillment?
- Passion?
- Druggery?
- Fair exchange?

Acronyms for JOB:

- Just Over Broke
- Jump Out of Bed
- Journey Of the Broke
- Just Out of Bondage
- Just Ordinary Business
- Just Obey Boss
- Jail Of Boss
- Journey Of Business
- Jump On Board
- Just On Board
- Join Our Bureaucracy
- Join Our Business

- Journey Of Borrowing
- Journey Of Brokeness
- Just Other's Business
- Just Old-enough to Borrow

Types of Employment:

- Unskilled labor
- Skilled labor
- Trade
- Union
- Non-union
- Contract employee
- White-collar profession
- Non-governmental business
- Government
- Administrative
- Maintenance
- Military
- Law enforcement
- Emergency service
- Self-employed
- Entrepreneur
- Politician

- Homemaker
- Farmer
- Rancher
- Healthcare

Status Levels of Professions:

No collar   -   Manual labor

Blue-collar   -   Skilled labor

White-collar   -   Administration/Management/Sales

Open collar   -   Owner/Entrepreneur

Disparities, Inequities, and Disproportions

Why people get paid so much or so little for what they do can be a mystery.

Socio/economic Questions:

Q: Why do sanitation workers make more money but have lower social status?

A: Fewer people are willing to do that type of work. (Hard, dirty work with negative status.)

Q: Why do most pastors make so little money but have high status?

A: High education level, influence, and leadership garner the status (Ideas of altruism and antimaterialism justify poor pay.)

Different types of vocations will provide different levels of psychological and sociological satisfaction and status.

When personal pride (or false pride) and considerations of social status need to be considered, lifetime dissatisfaction could occur in a career chosen for the wrong reasons.

Why?

Here are some rhetorical questions for you:

Why do people generally look down on:

- Mechanic
- Plumber
- Carpenter
- House painter
- Electrician
- Welder
- HVAC
- Sanitation
- Road maintenance
- Linemen
- Construction

Why do people generally admire and appreciate but still look down on:

- Police officers
- Firefighters
- Military
- Paramedics
- Nurses
- Bankers
- Attorneys

Why are doctors now being disrespected and having their pay limited?

Why do people look up to:

- Athletes
- Actors
- Musicians
- Models
- Celebrities
- Social media personalities
- Newscasters
- Politicians
- Teachers
- Ministers

Why do people look down on the very people who keep our entire world operating day in and day out? Shouldn't the people who build and maintain our infrastructure be admired as heroes?

Job Quality Factors:

Look for a job with these considerations in mind:

- Consistency/Stability of long-term employment?
- What industry/field appeals to you? Why?
- Could your lifestyle, health, and prosperity improve in a different region?
- Will there be career advancement and growth potential?
- Which careers offer long-term relevance to society?
- Could international competition undermine the success of your field of interest?

Career Questions:

- How long will it take to get your training?
- Can you afford to not earn for that educational period?
- How much will it cost to get that training?
- How much can you really expect to make?
- Will you truly recoup your education costs?

- What level of satisfaction will you enjoy?
- Can you tolerate that kind of work for 30 years?

Self-employment

"Being self-employed might be the highest form of wage slavery."

~Bert Wolfe

"Being self-employed isn't a career choice; it's a lifestyle choice."

~Stephen Liddell

Although I sometimes encourage some people to be self-employed, one must understand that most self-employed people work <u>far</u> more hours than other workers.

Advantages of Self-employment:

- Being your own boss.
- Taxation advantages.
- Discretionary use of your own time.
- Possibility of making a greater income.
- Pride in providing jobs.
- Possibility of controlling/creating wealth.

- It's a less tedious grind.
- More opportunities for creativity.
- Association with other prosperity-conscious people.
- You might enjoy the work.
- Providing valuable goods or services.
- Build assets to sell after time.

Disadvantages to Self-employment:

- Inordinate hours.
- Responsible for everything.
- Ass on the line - continuously.
- Endless employee problems.
- Employee turnover.
- Obsessive, compulsive dedication.
- Business takes priority over everything and everybody.
- High risk of setbacks and failures.
- Endless problems to solve.

The possibility of controlling your taxation and making more significant money is the draw, but you will spend way more time working. When your pay is divided by your hours, you may discover that you make more money per month, but your effective hourly pay rate is low. You can't get that time back. We must somehow spend less time making money.

And we especially need to spend less time doing things that don't fulfill us. If you decide to marry, have children, go to college, and commute, it all had better be mighty fulfilling. Otherwise, what is the point of all that effort? Do you think you will get a better place in heaven by being miserable? I doubt it.

I like to imagine that when we meet Saint Peter at the Pearly Gates for our entrance interview, he will pull up his clipboard and start asking questions like these:

1. Did you have fun?
2. Did you have a good adventure?
3. Did you get enough sex?
4. Did you enjoy your life?
5. Did you learn anything?
6. Did you serve your community?
7. Did you love anybody?
8. Did anybody love you?
9. Did you take care of yourself?
10. Did you get enough sleep?
11. Did you contribute anything?
12. Did you create any beauty?
13. Did you help anyone?
14. Would you do it again?

These are questions I *don't* think Saint Peter will ask:

- Did you work enough?
- Did you pay enough taxes?
- Did you give enough to the church?
- Did you impress your neighbors?
- Did you suffer enough?
- Did you prove somebody wrong?
- Did you make yourself right?

Manage the logistics of having a job.

How much money will you spend setting yourself up to make money?

- • Education

- • Continuing education

- • Networking

- • Wardrobe

- • Transportation

- • Time

- • Healthcare

Is spending on self-improvement paying off?

Making a Living

Socially <u>un</u>acceptable question:

"What do you do to make money?"

It's what we want to know, but it seems more polite to ask:

"What do you do for a living?"

Or simply:

" What do you do?"

People try to determine your socio/economic status level. It is human nature to sort everybody into a hierarchy of relative social positions. People become more comfortable when they get you *figured out*. Keeping them guessing and not fitting into their preconceived ideas can be fun.

Don't be surprised by people's constant attempts to pigeonhole you. They feel compelled to figure you out.

Hmmm, is he?

- Conservative?
- Liberal?
- Rich?
- Poor?
- Successful?
- Mediocre?

- Alpha?
- Beta?
- Beautiful?
- Frumpy?
- Handsome?
- Lumpy?
- Smart?
- Stupid?
- Ignorant?
- Glamorous?
- Unremarkable?
- Interesting?
- Insipid?
- Influential?
- Irrelevant?
- A nobody?
- Famous?
- Exciting?
- Boring?
- Dull?
- Memorable?
- Forgettable?
- Fascinating?
- Vapid?

Realize that you are constantly being sized up, so work to control the image of yourself that gets formed. Present yourself well physically and verbally. Use a well-practiced description of yourself, who you are, what you have to offer, and what you want.

What is the cost of making money? What do we spend in time and money to set ourselves up to make better money?

What is the cost of making your money?

- o Is your education strategically worth the costs?
    - ▪ Money?
    - ▪ Time?
    - ▪ Effort?
    - ▪ Earning delay?
    - ▪ Student loans?
    - ▪ Delayed earnings by being in school (years out of the workforce?)
- o Shoes and wardrobe (do not skimp)?
- o How expensive is your transportation?
- o Are you commuting?
- o Are you showing off with an expensive car?
- o Is there danger and risk on the job?
- o Overnight travel using up your personal time?

o   Prolonged absences from family?

o   Are you being paid enough for your sacrifices?

o   Is there undue psychological pressure?

o   Is there undue emotional stress?

o   Will you make enough more for these personal sacrifices to justify the costs?

Truism: "Do what you love."

Truth: Maybe. What you love must be valuable enough for someone to pay you well. Well-crafted buggy whips may no longer be a viable specialty.

Truism: "If you do what you love, you will never work a day in your life."

Truth: This truism has just enough truth to make it popular. The truth is that even if you love what you do, it will be work. You will still have to show up reliably and answer to bosses and customers, and you will still have to work. And it will still be a job. So, it had better be worth it. Doing what you love may be easier or more pleasant, but it may not pay the bills. The dream is to find something you feel compelled to do that also pays well.

Classic gag:

"When I was young, I was poor, but after years of hard work, I'm no longer young."

Chapter questions:

1. Will you make enough money to more than meet your most significant needs?
2. Can you afford an extra-ordinary life?

Conclusion: Sufficient money is fundamental to having an extra-ordinary life.

Chapter 9 Your Commute

Stress That Does Not Pay

The juice that ain't worth the squeezin'

"Contrary to Prediction of Equalization Location Theory, we find a large negative effect of commuting time on people's satisfaction with life."

~Alois Stutzer & Bruno S. Frey

Stress that Doesn't Pay: The Commuting Paradox

University of Zurich

Marginal Rate of Substitution: the cost of a good that a consumer is willing to trade for another good, as long as the new good is equally or more satisfying; An equation based on MRS theory. In economics, the **marginal rate of substitution (MRS)** is the rate at which a consumer is ready to give up one commodity in exchange for another.

"The costs of commuting far outweigh any valuation of benefits."

~Bert Wolfe

Costs of Commuting:

- $1 per mile[9]
- Personal time
- Insurance
- Tires
- Oil changes
- Washing, detailing
- Auto maintenance
- Auto repair
- Auto replacement
- Parking fees
- Tolls
- Being late
- Speeding
- Risk, hazard, danger
- Tickets
- General stress
- Bad weather

---

[9] $1 per mile times 100 miles times five days a week times 50 weeks equals $25,000.00.

- Stop and go
- Darkness
- Poor roads
- Other drivers
- Stress
- Additional hours of childcare

Read more: Marginal Rate of Substitution
http://www.investopedia.com/terms/m/marginal_rate_subst
itution.asp#ixzz4hH8f9Bu9

Opportunity Cost

Opportunity cost is the benefit, profit, or value of something that is given up to acquire or achieve something else. Since every resource (land, money, time, etc.) can be put to alternative uses, every action, choice, or decision has an associated opportunity cost. Opportunity costs are fundamental economic costs used to compute the cost-benefit analysis of a project. Typically, opportunity costs are not recorded in the account books but are recognized in decision-making by computing a given activity's cash outlays and time consumption. Does this project justify itself?

Lost Opportunity Cost

Potential money is lost when exterior forces like government regulations delay or prevent you from following through on economically fruitful endeavors.

Time-consuming activities have a cost that should be considered and calculated. Commuting has a significant *missed opportunity cost*. Most commuters foolishly fail to consider the value of the time they could be spending with their family and friends. Think of the vast activities that could be enjoyed in the hours spent commuting. A commuter could start a new business with the time wasted commuting. 4 hours x 5 days = 20 hours. That is half of full-time work!

Four unproductive hours per day, five days per week, and 52 weeks equals 1,040 hours of time wasted per year. Mind you, full-time is 2,080 hours. And don't bullshit me; calculate your time door to door, not city limit to city limit.

Mitigation

Please tell me you are using that time to do something that has value.

Mitigation Activities While Commuting:

- Podcasts
- Lectures
- Books read aloud

- Phone calls to all your friends and relatives
- Foreign language lessons
- Sleeping in your Tesla
- Thinking up ways to stop commuting

Cost-Benefit Analysis (CBA)

CBA quantifies the costs and benefits of a decision, program, or project (over a specified period) and those of its alternatives (within the same period) to have a single comparison scale for unbiased evaluation. Though employed mainly in financial analysis, a CBA is not limited to monetary considerations; It often includes environmental and social costs and benefits that can be reasonably quantified.

In my region, it is common for people to commute back and forth in snow storms over a treacherous mountain pass to an intensely trafficked city in order to live in a semi-affordable rural setting.

Long commutes probably contribute significantly to divorce. Commuting reduces home and family time, child time, intimacy time, and untold physical and mental tolls. From a dollar cost standpoint, commuting costs a fortune.

Questions About the Commute:

- Why do you live where you do?
- Is it the only place you know?
- Do you love it there?
- Strong economy?
- Strong job base?
- Esthetic community?
- Great lifestyle?
- Do friends and family live nearby?
- How do you get to and from work?
- Car?
- Bicycle?
- Bus?
- Train?
- Vanpool?
- How far is it - each way?
- Dangers on the road?
- Weather conditions – seasons?
- Why is it so far?
- How long does each journey take?
- Which is longer – to or from?
- What is the worst case?
- Is the commute time increasing?

- What geographical region?
- Climate?
- Snow?
- Ice?
- Topography?
- Mountain pass?
- Rural?
- Shoreline?
- Infrastructure?
- Roads in disrepair?
- Treacherous curves?
- Bumper-to-bumper congestion?
- Merging traffic?
- Cliffs?
- Narrow bridges?
- Tunnels?
- Salt rust?
- Tolls?
- Avoiding tolls?
- Parking?
- Culture?
- Aggressive drivers?
- Courteous drivers?

- Road rage?
- What do you drive?
- New?
- Used?
- Big?
- Small?
- Leased?
- Company?

Reasons people state in support of commuting:

- Better schools
- More pleasant living environment
- Safer neighborhoods
- Closer to friends or loved ones
- More affordable housing
- Quieter outside of the city
- Higher pay in the city

Benefits of Commuting:

- *Alone time* – if driving in a single-occupancy car.
- Personal time to work, play games, and nap – if riding a train or bus.

Consider this: Your car will eventually get out of warranty, and your maintenance and repair bills will double - or more.

Automobile Expense List:

- Insurance
- Registration
- Traffic tickets
- Break-ins
- Theft
- Gas
- Oil
- Tires
- Maintenance
- Repairs
- Accidents
- Collisions
- Stress/Health
- Mishaps
- Tolls
- Additional hours of childcare
- Parking fees
- Less time for:
  - Spouse
  - Kids
  - Friends
  - Hobbies
  - Sports
  - Sleep

It is not just the raw money cost of commuting; it's the time used.

Traffic congestion will do nothing but worsen.

Opportunity Costs

Opportunity costs are losses of potential gain from activities precluded by the alternate choices made. For example, idle cash balances represent an opportunity cost for lost interest.

Opportunity cost is the value of something lost when a particular course of action is chosen. Simply put, the opportunity cost is what you must forgo to get something. The benefit or value given up refers to decisions in your personal life, in a company, in the economy, in the environment, or on a governmental level.

Investors often use opportunity costs to compare investments, but the concept can be applied to many scenarios. If your friend chooses to quit work for a year to return to school, the **opportunity cost** of this decision is the year's worth of lost wages, strategic relationships, living expenses, books, and tuition.

Consider the *lost opportunity cost* of the time wasted on traveling to and from your job. That time could be used at your workplace or at home. Most people could have started a business or learned to play the piano with the time they wasted behind the wheel.

Commuting is a mental, physical, and psychological burden. If you sit down and do the math on commuting, you will see that commuting simply does not add up.

Counter to our culture, moving closer to your job is smarter. Most commuters gradually move farther and farther away from their job to pursue improved housing quality.

Advice: Find and stick with a job nearby that is good enough.

I have known people who have done reasonably well, having commuted for most of their careers. I believe only a very long consistency can make it pay. The open question is: how much more money could they have saved, and how much more enjoyment of life could they have had with all that time they spent commuting?

Commute Time Creep

- Increasing traffic due to increasing population
- Decreasing speed limits
- Additional stop lights
- "Traffic calming" additions like traffic circles, chicanes, and speed bumps
- You move farther from your job
- You drive less aggressively over time
- Increased law enforcement traffic control

Saving Time

You Need More Free Time

Why you need more free time:

- More sleep!
- More sex
- Leisure
- Exercise
- Sports
- Hobbies
- *Me-time*
- Yoga
- Family
- Kids

- Time to think

- Meditation

- Entertainment

- Altruism

- Moonlighting

- Housekeeping

- Household management

- Household improvement

- More time to do things right and thoroughly and properly, unlike the stuff we routinely short-cut when we are short of time

Extending your Commute

It is common for people to lengthen their commute repeatedly. Extending your commute is usually a financially illogical decision, particularly since commute times consistently increase over time in any decent job market. Nevertheless, people progressively move farther and farther from their jobs.

Chapter questions:

- What is your commuting strategy?
- How will you shorten and optimize the time wasted while getting back and forth to your job?

Conclusion:

- Avoid commuting
- Live near your work
- Make your travel time useful

Chapter 10: Your Housing

"The words home and house are not synonyms. A house is not necessarily a home. And a home is not necessarily a single-family house."

~Bert Wolfe

Type of Housing for You:

- Rent?
- Buy?
- Condo, Townhouse, House?
- Second House?
    - Why?
    - Where?
- Vacation house?

House versus Home

The words *home* and *house* are not synonyms. A house is not necessarily a home. And a home is not necessarily a single-family house.

A *Home* could be created within the following:

- A house
- A townhouse
- A condominium

- An apartment
- A room in somebody else's house
- A travel trailer
- A recreational vehicle
- A boat
- A tent
- A treehouse
- A cave
- A cardboard box

Your investment in a house will enjoy greater market appreciation the closer it is to the urban area. Market value is another reason to live nearer to your job in the city. Houses closer to job centers will naturally be more valuable, and people who can afford them have shorter commutes.

Reasons to Move:

- New
- Better
- Different

Negative Consequences of Moving:

- o Blown Efficiency Patterns
- o Need to build all new habits and routines
- o It is hard, time-consuming work
- o Relationship stress
- o Very hard on children (ACES)[10]

---

[10] **Adverse Childhood Experiences**

ACES: Adverse Childhood Experiences:

- Divorce
- Parental separation
- Moves
- Abandonment
- Abuse
- Humiliation
- Violence
- Neglect
- Missing or lacking parenting
- Parents fighting
- Alcoholism
- Sexual abuse
- Mental illness

o Lost good neighbors and friends
o Increased commute. Usually, people move farther away from work
o A different floor plan means buying new furniture and decor
o Bigger space means buying new furniture and decor
o The new yard needs fixing up (maybe it's a bigger yard or acreage)
o A new place will need fixing up
o Possibility of not liking the move

So many X-factors and Q-angles (inexplicable factors) are involved in making decisions like moving that it can be hard to stay practical and rational. You may have some intuitive need to move or an emotional/psychological need to move. But be clear about the reasons you are moving and the probable consequences.

Don't kid yourself with a reinforcing list of justifications for moving.

If you must move, then do it; just don't bullshit yourself with false and irrelevant justifications. Moving will be expensive

---

- Incarceration
- Suicide

and time-consuming, disrupting your established efficiency routines.

Get your moving done while you are young and less established. Strategically moving to an optimum region while younger could set you up for better success. Get yourself to a logical location, then stay put and build your life. Use your stable location as a foundational platform for success.

Moving? Really?

- Is it worth it?
- Will it substantially improve your life?
- Are you kidding yourself?
- Will your career advance?
- Will your marriage or prospects improve?
- Improved beauty and environmental esthetics?
- Improved lifestyle?
- Safer?
- Closer to loved ones?
- Closer to work?
- Do you need change?
- Are you restless?
- Escaping bad memories?

- Like-minded community?
- Better climate?
- Fresh and new digs?
- Improved socio-economic conditions?

Advice: Avoid housing churn.

Housing Lie: "You want to *own* your own *home.*"

Truths:

We rarely own a *home.*

Almost no one actually owns their dwelling. There is almost always a mortgage, which is a significant loan. Typically, people spend thirty years trapping capital in their residence by paying-in principle (capital) every month with the idea of someday having no house payment. Your money is trapped in your house because you need to live there; there is no investment income. That trapped capital is unlike a savings account because the money is illiquid. You can leverage money out of your house with periodic *cash-out* refinancing. If you pull money out of your house's capital, do so wisely; don't consume that money; only invest it. This is a topic for a whole other book.

Housing Lie: "Your house is your most   important investment."

The Truths:

Maybe:

- If you have invested in sweat equity improvements.
- If you have contracted remodeling and renovations.
- If regional market values have increased.

Your dwelling will rarely be a good investment.

For most people, it is simply a capital trap.

Market appreciation may occur, but that appreciation will do you no good if you sell and re-buy in the same market. You must sell high and move to a much cheaper market to enjoy appreciation.

The real estate commissions, closing costs, sales tax, capital gains tax, moving expense, furniture, and fix-up costs will often exceed any gain you may have made on the first house – especially if you re-buy in the same market. Don't kid yourself about this. If you can afford a bigger, better house, then so be it – but don't tell yourself that you enjoyed an equity gain. Most moves use up actual equity ratios.

You can periodically refinance your house with a home equity loan to capture that trapped capital if you are good with investing that capital. When carefully planned and timed, you can leverage market equity and sweat equity out of your dwelling – to invest in something more profitable – that *cash flows*.

It is better to choose an adequate dwelling, stay put, and

avoid trapping capital. That trapped capital will do you no good.

Rather than moving farther out for a better lifestyle, consider moving closer in for better economics. As your income increases, move closer. A closer-in house will gain market equity faster. Then, you can borrow (leverage) tax-free cash from your house and use it for investing.

The best advice is to live in your dwelling for the rest of your life.

When you qualify for a *reverse mortgage,* that may be your best move for optimizing cash flow and freeing your hard-earned capital.

Legitimate Reasons to Buy a House:

- Freedom to renovate
- The ability to write off interest may subsidize your *rent*
- A mortgage will effectively give you *rent control*
- Gradually build equity (although it will be trapped)
- A mortgage effectively forces you to park some of your own money rather than having it go to the landlord
- You can store up capital to use later in leveraging maneuvers
- You can access a reverse mortgage when you are old enough

Reasons not to buy a house:

- Much less responsibility
- More free time
- More flexibility to move, travel, and build a career
- Live closer to the job
- No maintenance and upkeep
- No renovations and improvements
- No property tax bills
- Renters insurance only
- You are not rooted down - limiting adventure

Chapter questions:

- What is your concept of an extra-ordinary life?
- Can you delay your luxury housing expenses?
- Can you build your finances first?

Conclusion: Examine all *conventional wisdom* regarding your housing. Avoid housing churn.

Chapter 11 Community

Community

Being a community member can provide feelings of fellowship with others due to sharing common values, interests, and goals.

A community comprises people who come together for a common purpose or goal, whether meeting like-minded people with the same interests or hobbies or exchanging information and opportunities. Typically, a community provides value to its members.

The word community is derived from the word common, which means having things in common.

Examples of Communities:

- Neighborhood Watch
- Home Owners Association
- Chamber of Commerce
- Board of Education
- Municipal
  o   Planning Commission
  o   City Council
  o   Parks Commission
  o   Design Review Board
  o   Public Safety Board

- Hospital Commission
- Veterans of Foreign Wars
- The Grange
- Political groups
- Service Clubs
  - Rotary International
  - Kiwanis
  - Lions Club
- Social clubs
- Country clubs
- Health clubs
- Church
- Bible study
- Book clubs
- Bridge club
- Professional associations
- Sports associations
- Car clubs
- Clubs of every kind

Community Service

Community service aims to help the community at the expense of your own time, without offering any compensation.

Examples of Community Service:

- Feeding the hungry
- Saving animals
- Cleaning up your neighborhood (community)
- Promoting Health and Safety
- Search and Rescue
- Service clubs
- The Red Cross
- Boy Scouts of America
- Girl Scouts
- YMCA
- Charitics of every kind

Conclusion:

Contributing your time, talent, and treasure to your community can be deeply rewarding, and it connects you to untold friendships, activities, and human resources.

Chapter 12 Stages of Life

Stages of Life

Lie: "Life is Long."

Wrong!

Life is short.

Life is short overall, and life occurs in stages - and the stages are short. And, to make life more intense, the stages overlap each other, so you can't devote yourself single-mindedly to any one stage. You will constantly (often desperately) juggle priorities across the endless demands of the *stages of life*. The longer you live, the more you will observe this.

In any given stage of life, you will feel like you don't have enough time, and life is whizzing by. If it is good, we think we have it made and operate like it's permanent. If it's terrible, we endure it and worry it is permanent. Of course, everything is transitory. Every moment is transitioning into something new. We can affect outcomes to some degree, but the constant is change.

So, get busy.

The idealized popular mythology of what a person wants to accomplish in their lifetime is unrealistic. To actually pull off a spectacular life – given all the responsibilities, barriers, constraints, accidents, acts of God, setbacks, and mistakes – you would need to live something like 400 years!

Don't waste time. Or, put more positively, optimize your time.

Strip out all wastes of your time:

- Useless activities
- Activities someone else could do
- Unnecessary obligations
- Unenjoyable habits
- Commuting
- Failures to delegate

We need to delegate more. We need to only do what only we can do. We need to delegate tasks that others can do. Only let yourself waste time in the most enjoyable ways possible. We can't be constantly productive, but we can avoid useless activities.

Life could seem long if you were:

- Bored
- Sick
- Suffer from chronic pain
- In a bad job
- Bad marriage
- Rotten lifestyle
- Terrible commute

The Basic and Overlapping Stages of Life:

- Birth and Infancy Stage
- The Childhood Stage
- The Coming-of-Age Stage
- The Education Stage
- Beginning Career Stage
- Faltering Career Stage
- Maybe on a Good Career Path Stage
- Dating Stage
- Looking for Spouse Stage
- Marriage Stage (congratulations)
- The Setting Up a Household Stage
- The Establishing a Personal Lifestyle Stage
- Procreation and Child Rearing Stage
- Employment and Career Development Stage
- The Career Building Phase
- Sophomoric Overconfidence Stage (commonly known)
- The Acquisition Stage (inevitable)
- Affluence Stage (hopefully)
- The Volunteer/Community Activist Stage
- Too Much Responsibility Stage
- Life is no longer Fun Stage
- Burnout and Dissatisfaction Stage

- The Failed Marriage Stage (hopefully not)
- The Midlife Crises Stage (hopefully not, but common)
- Struggling not to neglect what's left of your blown-up former family (yikes)
- Midlife Dating Stage
- Second Marriage Stage
- The Starting a New Family Stage (oh, no)
- The Spending Your Health for Wealth Phase (almost inevitable)
- Losing Your Parents Stage
- The Altruism and Charity Stage
- The Retirement Planning Stage
- The Working Longer Than You Want-To Stage (typical)
- The Grandkids Stage (can be fun)
- Life Gets More Expensive Stage
- The Denial of Aging Stage (standard)
- Will and Estate Planning Stage
- Attempts to restore estranged family and neglected friendships (worthy)
- The Retiring with Insufficient Resources Stage (all too common)
- The *Living on a Fixed Income* Stage (failure)

- The Travelling While You Are Still Kind-of-Young Stage (hurry up)
- The Returning to Work Stage (can be good for you socially)
- The Spending Your Wealth Restoring Your Health Stage (okay, so be it)
- Friends and Peers Are Dying Stage
- The Elderly Stage (with ease and grace)
- Losing Your Spouse Stage
- The Declining Health Stage
- Dying Stage
- Hospice Stage
- Death Stage

Keep in mind that these stages overlap and arrive out of sequence.

Managing the details of these phases and stages is a lot to pull off in just one short lifetime. Do we take on too much? Is it all worth it?

Small mistakes along the way amplify into catastrophic harmful effects.

In the middle of all these stages, we are trying to fit in:

- Getting enough sleep
- Exercise and physical fitness
- Healthy eating and lifestyle
- Preventative healthcare
- Mentoring children
- Devotion to our spouse
- Coordinating children's activities
- Attending children's events
- Personal fun and recreation
- Supporting each other's careers
- Maintaining and managing all your stuff
- Glamorous social life
- Love life
- Keeping up with *the Joneses*

The hell of it is you will never satisfactorily achieve these needs.

If you want to pull off a reasonably successful life, you had better think, plan, and choose wisely. You will not have time to waste fouling up your potential.

Conclusion: the sand is quickly running out of your hourglass.

Chapter 13 Midlife Crisis

"I once had a good employee who believed he needed to change something in his life – divorce, job change, car, house, whatever. I didn't want to lose him, so I caught myself hoping he would choose to get a divorce."

~Anonymous

Retired CEO

"All too often, a midlife crisis will trigger a divorce, which cascades into a financial disaster."

~Bert Wolfe

"The irony of the so-called midlife crisis is that it typically occurs during relative success and affluence. By the time a person has started to make it financially, they may be hitting a stage of burnout and dissatisfaction."

~Bert Wolfe

Elliott Jaques coined the term midlife crisis in 1965.

A **midlife crisis** could be described as faltering confidence and confusion regarding one's identity and self-confidence, often occurring during middle age or mid-career. A midlife crisis is typically preceded by a sophomoric period of nearly pathological confidence, which drives one into an era of relative success. This over-confident period leads to successes, failures, setbacks, and less success than expected, leading to frustration and disappointment. Fear of waning prowess may be present, and a person may become bored with a sustained period of seemingly monotonous or mediocre success. A midlife crisis is a psycho/emotional crisis brought about by events highlighting a person's growing age, inevitable mortality, and perceived lack of accomplishments. These perceived shortcomings may produce intense frustration, dissatisfaction, and anxiety. A desire to re-achieve youthful fun and adventure becomes strong. Drastic changes to one's lifestyle can lead to destructive actions that waste the hard work and sacrifice already invested in an extraordinary life. It is wise to view any sense of a midlife crisis as a predictable and routine stage of life. It is best to notice the feelings of the phase but retain your long-range focus.

Allowing a midlife crisis to spiral out of control is a classic way to destroy your plans to achieve and sustain an extraordinary life. Divorce is the most typical result of an out-of-control midlife crisis. Overspending on frivolous, ostentatious material goods and lifestyle is standard, as are dangerous pastimes.

The irony of a midlife crisis is that it typically occurs during relative success and affluence. By the time a person has started to *make it* financially, they may be hitting a stage of burnout and dissatisfaction.

The only path is to plow through and disregard the typical feelings of a mid-life crisis.

Minor lifestyle changes and improvements that are not disruptive could ease some of the dissatisfaction. It is essential to recognize that mid-life crises are predictable and are passing stages of a typical life.

Middle Age Crazy

By Jerry Lee Lewis

Today, he traded his big '98 Oldsmobile. He got a heck of a deal on a new Porsche car.

He ain't wearing his usual grey business suit. He's got jeans and high boots with an embroidered star.

And today, he's forty years old going on twenty. Don't look for the grey in his hair 'cause he ain't got any.

He's got a young thing beside him that just melts in his hand. He's middle-aged crazy, trying to prove he still can.

He's gotta woman that he's loved for a long, long time at home.

Ah, but the thrill is all gone when they cut down the lights.

They've got a business that they spent a while coming by. Been a long uphill climb, but now the profits are high.

But today, he's forty years old, going on twenty. And he hears of sordid affairs, and he ain't had any.

And the young thing beside him he knows she understands that he's middle-aged crazy trying to prove he still can

Oh, oh.

Source: LyricFind

Songwriters: Sonny Throckmorton

Middle Age Crazy lyrics © Sony/ATV Music Publishing LLC

"If there's a single lesson that life teaches us, it's that wishing doesn't make it so."

~Lev Grossman

A mid-life crisis could be triggered by aging or aging in combination with changes, problems, or regrets over:

- Career problems
- Marital relations (or lack of them)
- Maturation of children (or lack of children)
- Aging or death of parents
- Physical changes associated with aging

A mid-life crisis can affect men and women differently. The stereotype of a man going through a midlife crisis may include purchasing an exotic car or seeking intimacy with a younger woman. A man's midlife crisis is more likely to be caused by career issues. A woman's crisis may stem from confusion about her changing roles in the family as the children become more independent and eventually leave the household. Even though there are differences in why men and women go through a midlife crisis, their emotions can be intense.

Individuals experiencing a mid-life crisis may feel:

- A deep sense of remorse for goals not accomplished
- Fear of humiliation among more successful colleagues
- Longing to achieve a feeling of youthfulness
- A need to spend more time alone or with certain peers

- A heightened sense of your sexuality or lack of it
- Lethargy, confusion, resentment, or anger due to discontent with one's marriage, job, health, economic status, and social position
- Ambition to right the missteps taken earlier in life

Contributing to a midlife crisis can be a sense of burnout. Burnout comes when a person uses up their present time by trying to control future outcomes while avoiding painful mistakes and failures they have experienced in the past. So, pain from the past and fear of the future ruin the enjoyment of the present.

If your life is working well, don't change it. Enhance it, perhaps, but don't change it. Channel your dissatisfactions into building more power. Do not abandon your success formulas and habits due to transitory setbacks and petty dissatisfactions. Don't disconnect, don't stop communicating, and stay in contact with others. The first law of a condition of financial and social power is *don't disconnect*. Disconnection will bring about disaster for both you and anybody else involved. Be cautious of career changes and household moves; **don't get divorced**. Stay the course and get through it. A midlife crisis will pass; notice it, but don't do anything about it.

Note: This chapter is not meant to be a treatise on midlife crises, as I am only mentioning them because they can be a destructive phase of life.

The midlife crisis will pass.

In conclusion, a mismanaged midlife crisis could result in catastrophic setbacks to your plans for an extra-ordinary life.

Chapter 14 Time

Time

"Time waits for no one, and it won't wait for me."

~The Rolling Stones

"Time is money."

~Benjamin Franklin

"Manage your time; life is short!'

~Bert Wolfe

"Hours are like diamonds; don't let them waste."

~The Rolling Stones

"Time is money. Wasted time means wasted money."

~Shirley Temple

Great Lies About Life:

Lie: "There will be plenty of time for learning and mistakes."

Such a lie!

Life and time are always roaring forward. Life is a function of time and action. When you are in the learning phases, you had better make the most efficient use of time. Focus and target your learning tactically and strategically. Life constantly demands that we get on with it. We never have enough time to learn everything we need to know. We learn as much as possible until life grabs us and makes us participate. Once *participation* forces itself on us, hopefully, we will have learned enough and be clever enough to cope with whatever hits us next. Mistakes set you back in time and confidence. Avoid major mistakes. If we make a mistake, we must quickly analyze it for preventative purposes and immediately move on. There is no time for remorse, self-recrimination, or guilt. Make amends when appropriate and move forward.

Lie: "Love and family are more important than money."

This is a most reasonable and convincing lie. The most loving thing you can do for your family is to meet their needs. It takes lots of money on every level to accomplish this. In today's economy, being an impoverished parent does not cut it, and love does not make up for being broke.

Lie: "It is most important to love and enjoy what you do for a living."

That is great if you make enough to support the financial demands of your life. If people love their job so much, why do they want to win the lottery and retire?

Learn to value and respect work. Learn to make enough money to pay for your life. Here is a powerful sentence that doesn't make sense but is still profound: *"Work to afford things before you discover that you can't afford them."*

Lie: "Good Things Come to Those Who Wait"

Not in this universe! If you want good things to happen, then start making them happen. Be actively preparing for opportunities as they come and take them.

Lie: "It's better to be lucky than good."

"The phrase 'it's better to be lucky than good' must be one of the most ridiculous homilies ever uttered. In nearly any competitive endeavor, you have to be damned good before luck can be of any use to you at all."

~ Garry Kasparov

Deep Thinking: Where Machine Intelligence Ends and Human Creativity Begins

Two Good Lies:

- *"You need to be happy."*
- *"We are here to learn."*

The truth is that you need to serve. Life is hard work, and happiness is transitory at best. Satisfaction comes from competence, service, and accomplishment. We learn to be competent so we can be useful. The purpose of life is to serve.

"Might like to wear cotton, might like to wear silk. Might like to drink whiskey, might like to drink milk. You might like to eat caviar; you might like to eat bread. You may be sleeping on the floor, sleeping in a king-sized bed.

But you're gonna have to serve somebody (serve somebody), yes indeed. You're gonna have to serve somebody (serve somebody). Well, it may be the devil, or it may be the Lord. But you're gonna have to serve somebody."

~Bob Dylan

"Men credited with all kinds of ability, talent, brains, and know-how, including the ability to see into the future, frequently have nothing more than the courage to keep everlastingly at what they set out to do. They have that one great quality that is worth more than all the rest put together. They simply will not give up! When a man makes up his mind to do something, then it's only a matter of time. Staying with time takes bulldog persistence. This seems to be the entrance examination to success - lasting success -- of any kind!"

"Success is not the result of making money; making money is the result of success - and success is in direct proportion to our service."

~Earl Nightingale

How to Completely Change Your Life in 30 Seconds

Great Truths:

- Life is short
- Time is of the essence
- Life is expensive
- Children are expensive
- Health problems will occur

Life is Short, but Life is Long; the Great Dichotomy

Life is short:

Life feels long when we are children; then, life seems to accelerate to the point of anxiety and frustration, and then, life feels long again in old age.

The problem is that during young adulthood, we are so eager to grow up and get established that we scramble ahead with no real plan and try to do everything all at once: education, career, marriage, children, house, dog, cat, travel, etc. - all at once.

We tend to pile all the stages and phases of life on top of each other with no real plan.

Like everybody else, we dive in, scramble to cope, flounder, groping for success and satisfaction, and never really get organized. As we get through *middle age*, some dust settles, and suddenly, we feel old and washed up. It feels like we did what we could, but it didn't turn out as we dreamed, and now it's too late to do anything about it.

But life is long:

There are countless stories of people in their 60s, 70s, and 80s pulling off impressive late-life careers, accomplishments, and adventures. However, actuarial studies indicate that living long is statistically improbable, and that is why life insurance companies bet against you.

The problem for most people in the senior stage is that they are physically, mentally, and emotionally used up and burned out. It is a familiar story to see older people park themselves and idle out the rest of their lives—the long, slow goodbye.

"Since history began, humankind has struggled for survival. Survival can be as basic as food, water, shelter, sex, and safety. Once we meet the basic animal-level survival needs, humans need time for civilization, culture, love, and recreation. Most humans constantly seek satisfaction, meaning, status, love, belonging, and fulfillment. All of that takes a lot of time. We do not have time to wallow in our mistakes, misfortunes, and setbacks. We must not squander our time on useless pursuits."

~Bert Wolfe

Time is of the essence.

The personal activities I enjoy most require lots of money and time. *And* in addition to being expensive, these leisure activities take me away from working for money. In most families, making your living comes first, then family and church, then charity work, and finally personal time. Most people get very little personal free time. So, we need to be very efficient with our time and make good money in a concentrated fashion. And, occasionally, we need to devote time to just ourselves.

Sometimes, when I want to get off a phone call or turn down an invitation, I will joke that I will be otherwise engaged *"doing something critically relevant, with some very important people, at a significant location."* Or, *"I will be attending a magnificent soiree with glamorous people at an exotic venue."* Maybe I'm just going home to take a nap. It's fun to be silly about this, but the truth is, I tend to look at my time this way. Time is precious to me. Even if I am doing household chores, I try to be efficient so that I can goof off more.

My favorite pastimes are expensive in time and money:

- Quality love and sex life
- Active social life
- Breaking bread with friends and family
- Meditation
- Meaningful charity work
- Reading and studying
- Exotic sports
- Distant vacations

- Good Scotch and fine cigars
- Taking naps

When will you find time for:

- Lifelong learning?
- Self-improvement?
- Personal advancement?
- Attending church?
- Spiritual development?
- Charity/volunteer work?
- Fun social life?
- Strategic social life?
- Personal goals?
- Actual accomplishments?
- Serious sports?
- Significant hobbies?
- Bucket lists?
- New skills?

What you want is more time and money:

- To enjoy your life more
- To do amazing things
- To devote to your family
- More friendship time

- To make even more money
- To have a sideline business
- To *moonlight*
- To travel
- To learn new skills
- To build things
- To grow and expand

***Responsibilities* that seem to get in front of our *personal time*:**

- Career
- Extra-curricular business obligations
- Business trips
- Postgraduate training
- Spouse
- Children
- Parents
- In-laws
- Extended family
- Family, friends, and events
- Church
- Charity
- Home maintenance

- Auto maintenance
- Household chores
- Healthcare
- Exercise
- Social obligations
- Government compliance (IRS, DMV, etc.)

Note: None of the items on the above list get the time they need and deserve.

"All work and no play make Jack a dull boy."

That is so true, but remember that playing costs time and money. So, if you want to play as much as I do, you must optimize your earning potential and manage your time strategically. Being self-employed can be a way to have *discretionary use of your own time*, but it is often the path to more work hours than anybody else. Balance and boundaries are the keys. A balanced life is the most fulfilling life. You must compartmentalize your activities and allot time to your critical priorities. Create boundaries with your time and activities. Limit how much time you allot to work. *Work* never gets enough of you, and you never get ahead of work, so you must limit it. You must decide, bottom line, what is required to survive and not give more than that. Sure, occasionally, there are special projects, opportunities, and deadlines, but you must not make a habit of that; it will ruin your life balance. Balance is the key to a tolerable life.

We will never have enough time to pull everything off, which can be highly frustrating. We must evaluate how we spend our minutes, hours, and days. Cut out and seal off all activities and people who are chronic time wasters. Habitually consider how nonessential people waste your time.

Time Wasters

Unless you particularly enjoy the following activities or find them mentally therapeutic, decidedly limit them.

- Spectating professional and collegiate sports
- Thoroughly ingesting news sources
- Social media
- Commercial television
- Computer and cellphone games
- Non-strategic/unenjoyable social obligations
- Commuting
- Gossiping
- Keeping up with celebrities' lives

- Standing in lines
- Preparing and cleaning up meals at home
- Going to the grocery store every day
- Drinking too much alcohol
- Smoking cigarettes
- Getting sick
- Giving people more time than they deserve
- Habitually being tardy, late, and chronically *in a hurry*
- Misplacing your keys
- Losing your wallet
- Breaking, dunking, or losing your cell phone

Being in a Hurry

Observably, people who are chronically in a rush are time wasters. You will save time and stress by being early. You will be better composed when you arrive and produce better outcomes. It is most harmonious to be early. Stop trying to *optimize* your time. Most of us try to squeeze in as much activity as possible before breaking away and rushing to our next appointment or obligation. Being barely on time or late is disharmonious and spreads stress to others. Being on time is not the goal. Being early is the goal. Being early is truly being on time. Being early creates more harmonious outcomes.

Navy Seals have a famous saying, "Slow is fast."

Slow is smooth;

Smooth is fast,

So slow is fast.

Be Smooth

Maintain a smooth, unhurried pace, and be early to everything. You will be pleased with how much better things will turn out.

Upgrade your pastimes if you don't find them therapeutic, relaxing, and entertaining. Look at the word, *pastime.* Passing time! Are we simply passing the time, like wasting it or killing it? – until we run out of it for good? Or, can we use time and enjoy time? Maybe we can be more mindful of how we *spend* our time. If *time is money*, then like money, we should spend time wisely.

"Don't let the outside world dictate your mental input. Treat your subconscious well. Control the content of your input."

~Bert Wolfe

Control the Content of Your Input:

- Avoid broadcast/commercial television.
- Mentally filter your online news sources.
- Avoid commercial advertising.
- Stream wholesome content.
- Feed your mind with wholesome, intellectual input.
- Don't poison your mind with violent, degraded, and disharmonious input.
- Control the content of your conversations.
- Avoid gossip.
- Avoid controversy and arguments.
- Avoid stressful news that you can do nothing about.
- Avoid unpleasant *social obligations.*
- Avoid unsavory people, places, and events.
- Don't suffer fools.

Prevalent and insidious sources of negative input:

- Gossip
- Newspapers
- Magazines
- Broadcast television
- Poorly chosen media
- News services
- Radio shows

- Social media
- Video clips and *shorts*
- Some of your *friends*
- Some of your family
- Careless internet surfing
- Negative-minded business associates
- Negative minded co-workers
- Government agencies

"Control the content of your input."

~Bert Wolfe

Be aware of psychological impediments to your momentum.

Introverting Confidence Killers:

- Guilt trips
- Disappointments
- Failed romance at home
- Created intimacy somewhere else
- Missed many kids' events
- Not that good of a friend
- Career stalled
- Neglected aging parents
- Lost touch with old friends
- Neglected siblings
- Vacations were not relaxing

- Neglected personal interests
- Neglected sports and exercise
- Gotten out of shape
- Gained weight
- Business trips don't count as *traveling*
- Too tired to enjoy anything

Allow for Serendipity

Serendipity: the occurrence and development of events in a happy or beneficial way.

Leave room in your planning to allow fortuitous serendipity to enter the equation.

A caution regarding overplanning: Don't plan with such rigidity that you preclude serendipity. Serendipity is what happens when good planning and preparation meet opportunity. Keep your plans fluid and adaptable.

Serendipity is the essence of luck; after planning and preparing, it sets the stage for action.

Recap of Essential Time Management Principals:

- Life is Short.
- Life will deliver setbacks.
- There is little time to get back on track.
- There will be few *do-overs*.

- There is no time to wallow in loss.
- Get beyond major mistakes early in your life.
- Don't hurry while in your youth.
- Don't waste time in midlife.
- Forethought and consistency rule the day.
- Think and consider before you choose, act, or decide.
- Be cautious about *following your heart*.
- Look before you leap.
- Be afraid of falling (in love).

Personal Time

How much personal time do we get each day? Very little. We need to sleep 8 hours each night. We need an hour to prepare for bed and wake up. Let's call that 9 hours. Another 3 hours for food procurement, preparation, eating, and clean-up. Two hours for exercise, grooming, and personal time. Now we're at 14 hours.'

How would you spend your precious coins if each hour were a gold coin that you could never get back?

How many hours does a workday require?

8 - sleep

1 - prep for bed and waking up

1 - personal body care

2 – commutes, including transporting children to school

and/or childcare

9 - work

3 – meals

2 - household chores and maintenance

1 – errands, coffee with a friend, or doctor's appointment

1 – exercise or gym

1 - wind-down at home

1 - management of children

1 - family time

1 – spouse time

Thirty-two total hours – oops!

8 hours short!

So, given only 24 hours, which activities get shorted? Sleep gets shorted the most, which severely affects your health and your enjoyment of life. Countless studies have verified the tremendous importance of getting 8 to 8.5 hours of sleep.

The second thing you will short is time with your spouse. What is the point of any of your life set-up if it all blows up in divorce?

How will your career go if you short work?

Are you willing to be an absentee parent?

You can short everything on the list except for the commute. The commute will be whatever it is, varying and invariably increasing over time.

Most people commute more than two hours a day. You can see that the most heinous use of time is transporting your body to work and back daily.

You can't shorten your commute, so you must short everything else. Look at the items on this simple list. It is not good to short any of these things.

And you can easily see you will get no personal time.

The only way to successfully survive this daily time conundrum is to have a flexible job and a short commute. Otherwise, you will be a typical burned-out, divorced, indebted, frustrated, wage-earning tax slave - for your entire adult life.

Parents are constantly guilt-tripping themselves about missing their children's games and recitals, but how can the parent help it?

"And you run, and you run to catch up with the sun, but it's sinking.

Racing around to come up behind you again
The sun is the same in a relative way, but you're older.

Shorter of breath and one day closer to death

Every year is getting shorter, never seem to find the time

Plans that either come to naught or half a page of scribbled lines

Hanging on in quiet desperation is the English way.

The time is gone, the song is over, thought I'd something more to say."

~Pink Floyd

Time

"I ain't wasting time no more. Because time goes by like hurricanes and faster things."

~Gregory Allman

"There's only one thing more precious than our time, and that's what we spend it on."

~Leo Christopher

Conclusion: Time is money. Make enough time to create the extra-ordinary life of your dreams.

Chapter 15 Financial Planning

Finances

"Life is Change."

~Donald Trump

"Life is change. And change is expensive."

~Bert Wolfe

"Life is change

And change is changing."

~Unknown

Most people dislike change. People fear change for two reasons:

- Fear of losing something they like.
- Fear of getting something they don't want.

We must learn to accept change and to manage change readily and effectively.

Worldwide, the rate of change is accelerating. Change is coming in faster and faster waves. The changes in our world are more enormous with each passing year.

We are living in a new era.

Since change is inevitable, we would be wise to anticipate it and not be surprised and shocked by it. Many are disoriented by change and are slow to adopt new ways.

Personal technology is advancing at an incredible pace. You must adopt it or be left pathetically behind.

Trappings of a Technology Loser (AKA: a *late adopter*):

- Rolodex
- Day Planner
- Landline at home
- Cable TV
- Flip Phone
- Briefcase
- Filing Cabinets
- Answering Machine
- Maps and Thomas Guides
- Compact Discs
- DVDs
- Cellphone in hand while driving
- House keys

Develop foresight and begin to predict the details and timing of changes coming your way.

When major change arrives, you must be ready with a solid game plan and adequate finances.

Conventional wisdom tells you to:

- Make a good salary
- Buy everything at wholesale
- Achieve 5-8% on investments

Unconventional Practice:

- Earn Money.
- Spend significantly less than you earn.
- Save substantial emergency reserves.
- Never invest your emergency funds.
- Keep your emergency funds liquid and never at risk.
- Keep building your emergency funds.
- Then, build up substantial investment capital.
- Invest your capital consistently, based on an unvarying philosophy.

We are not taught to avoid financially catastrophic mistakes. The losses and setbacks from big mistakes hugely outweigh the positive gains from conventional money management theories.

Classic comic story:

I addressed a high school life planning course shortly after retirement. I talked about staying in school, getting good grades, and all that usual bullshit, then I threw it open for questions. One student asked, *"Can you give us any financial advice?"* I said, *"Sure; looking back over my 6-plus decades, I believe I've spent close to 90 percent of my earnings on booze and whores. The rest, I just pissed away."*
They escorted me out before getting to share my two rules to live by:

1) If it flies, floats, or fucks, it's cheaper to rent it!

2) If it's got tits or tires, you'll have problems with it. I hope they invite me back next year so I can finish. **Kids need to know this stuff.**

Moral: It is essential to allow yourself rewards and luxuries along the way to your financial success.

Excessively depriving yourself now of riches tomorrow could ruin the fun of today's game of success.

As you begin to succeed, you want to bolster your knowledge and skills by paying for coaching, training, tools, and facilities that increase your career and business prowess.

You also need to maintain a balanced lifestyle rather than becoming a *workaholic*.

So, how much fun, adventure, and luxury should we afford?

Only you can decide, but at least sometimes, you must consider the true costs. Will you get enough satisfaction from spending that money to justify the expense? "Is the *juice* worth the *squeeze*?" Could you enjoy and be satisfied by spending less time, money, and risk?

Could you get similar juice for less squeeze:
- Backpacking instead of hotels and car rentals?
- Mountain biking instead of motorbiking?
- Local car vacations instead of airplane trips to exotic locations?
- Better furnishings in a modest house.
- Better quality but less stylish clothing and shoes.
- Well-maintained modest car rather than a prestigious car.
- Quality food at home rather than gourmet restaurants?

Expensive Habits:
- Commuting
- Poor health habits causing chronic sickness and disease
- Spending your health to gain wealth
- Credit card and consumer debt
- Bad Luck and Trouble

- o https://www.youtube.com/watch?v=xH_Z8xb2g vs

- o   https://youtu.be/8uK88d0 yf_Q?si=p-zxGskDxHNHVJl3

- Cavalier safety awareness
- Watching commercial broadcast television!!!

A careless accident could cause you to lose everything you have worked so hard for.

Stop pissing away your life watching low-grade broadcast television. You must decidedly and strategically control the quality and quantity of your input to your brain.

Catastrophic Financial Disasters

- *Unplanned* Children

  - o *"If you fail to plan, you are planning to fail!"*

    ~ Benjamin Franklin

- *Accidental* children
- Marrying the wrong person
- Divorce
- Being fired or laid off
- Frequently changing your living quarters
- Repeatedly changing careers
- DWI, DUI

- Arrest and Prosecution
- Losing a legal suit
- Vehicle engine failure
- Major theft
- Financial fraud
- Serious illness
- Severe injury – disability
- Natural disaster
- Significant *accidental* loss of possessions
- Extra-marital affairs
- IRS problems

A substantial safety net of liquid emergency money is essential in life.

Having More than Enough Money:

- Enhances quality-of-life
- Reduces stress levels
- Improves health levels
- Increases enjoyment and pleasure
- Provides peace of mind
- Avails freedom
- Promotes adventure
- Solves problems
- Helps others

- Creates beauty
- Facilitates romance
- Amps up fun

Financial Independence:

- More income than outgo
- Enough to live on for life
- Substantial ability to borrow
- Alternative sources of income
- Thoroughly insured
- No debt of any kind
- No partners
- No dependents
- Able to handle any medical expense

Being financially free is a fun and worthy goal, but it is probably unrealistic for most people. Most people who approach this level are naturally enterprising, so they will invest with "investment capital" and have partners and often some investment debt. These people will usually have other people relying on them in some way or another.

The point is that you can better serve your greater purposes when you are financially free.

People have told me they live faith-based lives and that making children is more important than making money.

My response is that if you manage your finances better, you will have more time and money to spend on raising your children – with emphasis on raising. Children are not pets for your enjoyment. They must be raised, elevated to a higher position or level, and lifted. To be raised means to be developed, brought up, and nurtured; To be taught during childhood to exhibit good manners and pleasant behavior (well-mannered, well-behaved, polite, civilized, polished, and refined.)

If you truly believe that God expects you to have many children, then you had better figure out how to afford to take good care of them – at a minimum of 500K each.

A person might say, "God will provide." Well, God is busy elsewhere and leaves child rearing to the breeder.

When churches promote procreation, I have to wonder if they are more interested in creating more tithers than the welfare of families.

The Three Worst, Most Common Financial Habits:

Changing Houses, Spouses, and Careers.

- Changing Houses:
    - Moving disrupts efficiencies.
    - The expenses of moving:
        - Time, time, time, time, money, effort, and time.

- Changing spouses.
- Changing Careers.
  - Avoid repeatedly changing careers. I do not mean that changing employers is necessarily a bad habit. Certainly, you want to progress.

Expensive Actions and Situations:

- Stalled Careers:
  - Be wary of the title-advance flim-flam used by big banks and big box stores. They give you a new, more impressive title and a tiny raise. Employers sometimes exploit employees by using the psychology of making them feel like they are advancing in their careers while their income-earning growth gets stunted. You might get advanced to Senior Vice President of Stalled Advancement. You get to tell your spouse and your mother that you got an advancement at work, but that is about all the good it does you.
- Poor health habits and disease.
- Excessive Acquisitiveness.
- Severe Injury or Death.
- Getting Grifted: theft, fraud, embezzlement, gold diggers, bait and switch, con, etc.
- Joining a cult.

Overlooked Financial Drains and Impediments:

- Commuting
- Parking
- Poor grammar
- Lack of etiquette
- Poor table manners
- Unfortunate accents
- Too much self-expression
- Lower-class body language
- Poor posture
- British teeth
- Bad haircuts
- Out-of-style clothes
- Cheap-looking clothes
- Ill-fitting, untailored clothes
- Cheap shoes (inexcusable)
- Correctable cosmetic problems
- Too stylish (foppish)
- Hair and lash extensions
- Extreme fingernails (raptor claws)
- Excessive makeup

Simple Financial Advice:

- Get a strategic education
- Groom and dress well
- Learn good manners
- Build your grammar and vocabulary
- Strategically build and advance your career
- Marry wisely
- Avoid divorce
- Procreate wisely
- Minimize commuting
- Get a good house and stay put
- Optimize your time
- Live a moderate lifestyle
- Learn how to be lucky
- Choose your people carefully
- Take care of the people who take care of you
- Study this book repeatedly

Competitive Materialism

Beware of wasting resources competing socially and financially. There are no shortcuts, and you will only look pathetic trying to pose as more than you have yet achieved.

The concept of "Fake it 'till you make it" has some workability but only incrementally and if carefully orchestrated. Promoting (positioning) yourself is a valid exercise in principle, but it can backfire into making you look like a jackass. There is a fine line between positioning and showing off. Materialistic competition is a fool's game.

Subtle and overlooked financial drains and impediments:

- Commuting
- Pay Parking
- Daily fancy coffee
- Poor grammar
- Poor table manners
- Unfortunate accents
- Unrepaired cosmetic problems:
  - Bad wardrobe
  - Bad teeth
  - Bad haircut
  - Facial hair
  - Bad breath
  - Bad hygiene
  - Obesity
  - Birthmarks
  - Poor image
  - Poor health
  - Poor mobility

- o Stinginess
- o Social awkwardness
- Too much self-expression
  - o Extreme hair
  - o Tattoos and piercings
  - o Unconventional clothing
  - o Extreme language
  - o Gratuitous swearing
  - o Jokes of poor taste
  - o Too much animation
- Cable television (plus other feeds)
- Failing to change your oil
- Fancy cars
  - o https://www.youtube.com/watch?v=Eu13NFEigPw
- Chronic lateness
  - o ***"Early is on time, on time is late,***
    and late is unacceptable!"
    ~Eric Jerome Dickey
- Being in a hurry
- Speeding
  - o Dangerous
  - o Expensive tickets
  - o Increased insurance premiums
- Drunk driving

- Poor health habits
- Artificial sweeteners
- Extreme religion

"Church on Sunday, sleep and nod, trying to duck the wrath of God. Preachers filling us with fright. They all trying to teach us what they think is right. They really got to be some kind of nut (I can't use it.) Trying to make it all real —but compared to what."

~Gene McDaniels

Compared to What · Composer

- Poor personal security habits
- Expensive hobbies
- Expensive vices
    - Partying
    - Gambling
    - Hookers
- Illicit habits and activities
- Illegal activities.
- Expensive travel
- Expensive collections
- Exotic entertainment
- Depression
- Friends who are not friends

Vices

Vices can lead to addictions. Addictions ruin lives.

Beware of excessive:

- Food
- Drink
- Substances
- Gaming
- Gambling
- Sex

Call girls are cheaper than wives. But being *busted* by your wife or the police can be very expensive and distracting.

In most of America, it is best to restrict sex to dating or marriage.

Disability expense:

- Eldercare
- Disabled children
- Disabled spouse
- Personal disability

Expensive Sports

- Auto racing
- Private flying
- Motorcycling
- Golfing

- Skiing
- Shooting sports

Dangerous Sports

(Higher Odds of Severe Injury or Death)

1. Cave diving
2. Base jumping
3. Paragliding
4. Private flying
5. Auto racing
6. Motorcycling
7. Mountain climbing
8. Backcountry skiing
9. Street and highway bicycling
10. Rock Climbing
11. Scuba diving
12. Sky diving
13. Snowmobiling
14. Mountain Bicycling
15. Inbounds Skiing
16. Backcountry skiing
17. Contact sports (basketball, hockey, soccer, etc.)

If you insist on doing some of these dangerous activities, then for God's sake:

- Get highly trained
- Be very fit
- Practice regularly
- Use only the best and latest equipment
- Participate with experts only
- Know your limits
- Practice, train, and rehearse

Expenses you should eliminate:

- Landline Telephone
- Cable Television Packages (Wi-Fi only)
- Weekly lawn care (xeriscape)
- Watering the lawn (xeriscape[11])
- Swimming pool (hot tub only)

Changing and Churning: Spouses, Houses, and Careers

Most Common Financial Mistakes:

1. Unplanned children
2. Divorcing
3. Moving
4. Career hopping
5. Commuting
6. Addictions

Catastrophic Financial Disasters

- *Unplanned* children
- Divorce

---

[11] Xeriscape is a type of landscape design that reduces and minimizes irrigation. Save time, water, chemicals, and money by converting your lawn and landscape plantings to xeriscape.

- Poor health habits creating chronic sickness and disease
- Extreme acquisitiveness
- Severe Injury or death
- Uninsured loss
- Theft
    - Getting grifted
    - fraud
    - embezzlement
    - gold diggers
    - robbery
    - burglary
- Addiction

Excessive Financial Drains

- Fancy cars
- Expensive hobbies
- Expensive sports
- Expensive vices
- Expensive travel
- Expensive collections
- *Going out* drinking

Overlooked Expenses:

- Cable television (could easily add up to $3,000.00 per year) (Recommend WIFI only. No landline.)
- Not changing your oil (frequent oil changes will save you a fortune in a car you plan to keep; consequences: $8-10K for a blown engine)
- Blown engine due to overheating:
  - Low coolant
  - Failure to watch the temperature gauge

Pets and Vets

In today's world, pets are family and treated like children. Veterinary care has become very specialized. Extreme injuries and exotic illnesses can often be successfully treated – at great expense. Pets are no longer treated like farm animals that were readily replaced in the event of even minor problems. Those days are gone, and pets are *costly*. Don't kid yourself; an unexpected vet bill could cause a severe financial setback.

Kenneling fees are an overlooked expense. When you travel without your dogs, figure that kenneling fees for two dogs will run about the same as lodging for yourself.

Realistically, we should financially plan for our pets as we do for children. Pets' lifetimes last about half the twenty to thirty years of human children staying in the house, and pets don't go to college; nevertheless, pet expenses must be budgeted. Pet expenses are high enough to delay your financial progress significantly.

Pet insurance is probably a good idea for the likely event of a catastrophic veterinary expense.

Pets also require a lot of your time. In the name of the humane treatment of animals, please don't get a pet if you won't have daily time to devote to them.

Competitive Materialism

- The cost of keeping up with the Joneses is too high. Don't compare yourself to others.
- The cost of establishing and projecting your socioeconomic status is too high.
- (Until you authentically live and operate at a high socioeconomic level, I advise you not to try.)

The status level you want to project would be expensive enough to delay your financial goals. This is one instance when you can't effectively *fake it until you make it.*

Know where you are, focus on where you want to be, and imagine how it will feel when you get there.

Tithing: 10%

Tithing to a church may not be your most effective generosity.

Could your generosity be better allocated?

Could contributions be better spent directly on specific charities of your choice?

Do you believe your church achieves the kinds of outcomes you believe in?

Design and Establish Your Lifestyle:

- Avocations
- Leisure
- Hobbies
- Sports
- Toys
- Travel
- Volunteer work
- Indulgences
- Vices
- Religion

Making your Vocation into your Avocation - Loving What You Do for Dough - Versus: Loving What Your Dough Does for You.

You may need to save the dream of loving your work until you are financially secure enough to transition into retirement. In the meantime, find a way to make what you do for money feel worthy of your time and talent.

"Prepare for the unforeseen. Maintain an emergency account - a financial safety net. Be prepared."

~Bert Wolfe

Investing

Knowledge and timing set up luck by aligning with random opportunities. Opportunities are not entirely unpredictable, given good knowledge and experience. However, opportunities must be prepared for, based on the philosophy that they will come randomly. So, stage yourself for good luck.

Random: happening without a method or definite plan.

"Well, I'll be ready now.

I'll be ready when my train pulls in.

Oh, I'll be ready now.

Oh, I'll be ready when my train pulls in, yeah."

~Gary Clark, Jr.

Conclusion: Manage your finances to support the extraordinary life of your dreams.

Chapter 16 Your Life Plan

Policies, Plans, and Procedures

"Living by default is operating indiscriminately with no plans or policies, winging it and getting default results."
~Bert Wolfe

Your Life Plan, Guiding Principles, and Unshakable Values

Elements of a Plan

- Targets
- Goals
- Destination
- Purpose
- Details
- Consistency

Guiding Principles

Guiding Principles frame the details of the Plan.
You need a detailed plan, but thorough planning takes time, and the plan is continually being adjusted and tuned.

To maintain consistency in your planning, you need guiding principles that don't change over time.

Unshakable Actions:

- Establish policies.
- Implement procedures.
- Live by codes of conduct.
- Develop guiding principles.
- Operate on formulated values.
- Exercise developed taste.

Unshakable Values

A stable plan is built on foundations of unshakable values.

Unshakable values:

- Honesty
- Integrity
- Code of Honor
- Sanity
- Clear thinking

Poverty

There are many types of poverty:

- Financial deficiency poverty
- Lack of emotional stability poverty
- Unfulfilling relationships poverty
- Lost and inconsistent Love
- Failed and lost personal connections
- General state of dissatisfaction
- Lack of personal fulfillment
- Lack of self-awareness
- Insufficient education
- Lack of social graces
- Poor health
- Poor self-esteem
- Poor self-image
- Social awkwardness
- Poor grammar
- Lack of manners
- Lack of integrity
- Poor ethics
- Poor grooming
- Negative attitude (poor attitude)
- Poor planning
- Thoughtlessness

- Poor health
- Poor grooming
- Bad teeth
- Poor posture
- Poorly dressed
- Selfishness (lack of love)
- Immorality (lack of principles and honor)
- Poor judgment (lack of common sense)
- Promiscuity (no true love)
- Bad luck (lack of good fortune)
- Ungrounded (no home, no roots)
- PTSD (too much harm, too much loss)
- Fatigue (lack of energy)
- Poverty consciousness (belief in excessive success for others, belief in shortages) (belief in limited resources and that some people have too much)
- Stinginess (not enough for me; I got mine, now screw you)
- Chronic lateness (insufficient time, lack of planning, poor planning)
- Critical of others (lack of empathy and compassion)
- Negative self-talk (lack of confidence, poor self-esteem)

Sin: The Latin meaning of the word sin is *without* (God, guidance, principles.) Poverty of spiritual, moral, and ethical guidance.

So, it could be said that it is a sin to be without a plan, a code of honor, and financial success.

Dreams and Plans Can Have Conflicting Goals

For example:

- I want to live a simple country life, but I want to be a successful corporate attorney.
- I want to raise a family, but I want to be a touring musician.
- I want to be a world-class athlete, but I want to be a neurosurgeon.
- I want to be a priest, but I want a wife. I want to be a nun, but I want a husband.
- I want to be a man, but I am a woman. I want to be a woman, but I am a man.
- I want to be rich, but I have no gumption.
- I am lazy, but I want to be rich.
- I am shy, but I want to be respected.

Examples of codes of honor, oaths, and codes of conduct:

- ❖ Scout Oath
- ❖ Scout Law
- ❖ Military Oath
- ❖ Medical Creed
- ❖ Oath of Office
- ❖ Police Officers Oath
- ❖ The Cowboy Way
- ❖ The Code of the West
- ❖ Professional Codes of Conduct
- ❖ Medical Oath
- ❖ Ten Commandments
- ❖ Ragger's Creed
- ❖ Religious Creeds
- ❖ Codes of Honor
- ❖ Polite Good Manners

Creed: a set of beliefs or aims that guide someone's actions; a statement of a community's shared ideas in a form structured by subjects that summarize its core tenets.

Why would anyone swear an oath? Why all these rules, codes, laws, and commandments?

You need to answer these questions for yourself.

Free Agency (Moral Agency; Free Will)

Humans are not machines. We are born with free will and religious free agency, so we don't have clearcut innate codes of conduct and guidelines built into our brains. To some degree, most of us have a conscience, but we need to learn habits of good social behavior.

Humans are born with the freedom to perpetrate evil (sin.) The overriding influences are laws, moral codes, and, to some degree, an innate *conscience*.

Conclusion: You cannot have the extra-ordinary life of your dreams without a life plan based on specific guiding principles of personal behavior.

Chapter 17 Luck, the Making Of

Make Yourself Lucky

"Preparation is the essential element of having good luck."

~Bert Wolfe

We make our own luck.

For the most part, we make our own luck.

If we have no plan, have no personal policies, and don't prepare for anything, we get what?

We get bad luck.

We mostly have good luck when we make detailed plans, have clear personal policies, and specifically prepare for opportunities.

I am acquainted with many Eagle Scouts. Eagle Scouts are consistently lucky and successful. These Scouts learn specific success principles, habits, codes, and rules to live by.

The entire purpose of Scouting is to shape kids into ethical, successful, exemplary young people.

The strongest influence in my life is the model of the Boy Scouts of America. The following are the fundamentals of Scouting.

The Scout Motto:

"Be Prepared"

It is much less likely you will have bad luck when you have taken the trouble to be prepared. When you are prepared, you can take advantage of opportunities; when you are prepared, you will more likely be able to solve problems as they arise.

Preparation is the essential element of having good luck.

The *luckiest* group of people I know are Eagle Scouts.

Eagle is the highest rank in scouting.

Eagle Scouts have accepted and pledged to particular guidelines to live their lives.

The Scout Oath:

*"On my honor, I will do my best to do my duty to God and my country and to obey the **Scout Law**. To help other people at all times, to keep myself physically strong, mentally awake, and morally straight."*

The Scout Law:

A scout is:

- Trustworthy
- Loyal
- Helpful
- Friendly
- Courteous
- Kind
- Obedient
- Cheerful
- Thrifty
- Brave
- Clean and
- Reverent

Boy Scout Slogan:

"Do a Good Turn Daily"

A comprehensive list of skills must be mastered through a series of ranks to achieve Eagle. What sets the rank of Eagle apart from the lower ranks is the requirement to demonstrate significant leadership and community service.

Leadership

The required leadership of your own life:You must be the leader of yourself

- The leader of your own life
- The leader of your career
- The leader of your family
- The leader of your future

Eagle Scouts are not lucky by accident. They have set up their lives to be lucky.

Scout Motto: Be Prepared

Being prepared requires forethought. We need to think ahead. With good preparation, our luck is set up. When we are prepared, we have better foresight. We start having better predictions about probable outcomes. We see things coming – both good and bad.

People often ask me, "How did you know?"

Elements of Accurate Prediction:

- Forethought
- Planning
- Preparation
- Acquired knowledge
- Personal experience

- Learning from others
- Foresight
- Keen observation
- Active involvement in your field of endeavor
- Positioning yourself in the proximity of opportunities
- Being there
- Being there
- Being there some more

Rotary International Mottos:

- "Service Above Self"
- "One Profits Most Who Serves"

Rotary International Four-Way Test:

1. Is it the truth?
2. Is it fair to all concerned?
3. Will it build goodwill and better friendships?
4. Will it be beneficial to all concerned?

"I'm a great believer in luck, and I find the harder I work, the more I have of it."

~Thomas Jefferson
3rd President of the United States

Statesman, Diplomat, Architect, Philosopher

Founding Father

"Remember that sometimes, not getting what you want is a wonderful stroke of luck."

~Dalai Lama XIV

"Shallow men believe in luck or in circumstance. Strong men believe in cause and effect."

~ Ralph Waldo Emerson

"Luck has a way of evaporating when you lean on it."

— Brandon Mull, Keys to the Demon Prison

"Ability is of little account without opportunity."

— John Miltonpoléon Bonaparte

"Some luck lies in not getting what you thought you wanted but getting what you have, which once you have

it, you may be smart enough to see is what you would have wanted had you known."

— Garrison Keillor, Lake Wobegon U.S.A.

"Concentration attracts luck factor."

— Amit Ray, Yoga and Vipassana: An Integrated Life Style

"Life is not easy. We all have problems-even tragedies-to deal with, and luck has nothing to do with it. Bad luck is only the superstitious excuse for those who don't have the wit to deal with the problems of life."

— Joan Lowery Nixon, In The Face of Danger

"People always call it luck when you have acted more sensibly than they have."

— Anne Tyler

"Luck is the residue of design."

— John Milton

"The harder I work, the luckier I get."

— Samuel Goldwyn

"I am a great believer in luck, and I find the harder I work, the more I have of it."

— Stephen Leacock

"I've found that what most people call luck is often little more than raw talent combined with the ability to make the most of opportunities."

- Timothy Zahn,

Heir to the Empire

"Do you wait for things to happen, or do you make them happen yourself? I believe in writing your own story."

— *Charlotte Eriksson*

"Were you looking for a horseshoe?"
"No, I was expecting the horse, but the shoe is a piece of pure, gorgeous luck."

— *Dorothy L. Sayers, Have His Carcase*

"You know, if you're an American and you're born at this time in history especially, you're lucky. We all are. We won the world history Powerball lottery."

— *Bill Maher*

"Luck was fine and well, but I didn't need it. I had a plan."

— Kiera Cass, Happily Ever After

"There are rules to luck; not everything is chance for the wise; luck can be helped by skill."

— Baltasar Gracián, The Art of Worldly Wisdom

"The deadly sin is to mistake bad play for bad luck."

— Ian Fleming, Casino Royale

"I may say that this is the greatest factor: the way in which the expedition is equipped, the way in which every difficulty is foreseen, and precautions taken for meeting or avoiding it. Victory awaits him, who has everything in order; luck, people call it. Defeat is certain for him who has neglected to take the necessary precautions in time; this is called bad luck."

~ Roald Amundsen

Polar Explorer

"Learn to recognize good luck when it's waving at you, hoping to get your attention."

~ Sally Koslow

Author

"Good luck is a residue of preparation."

~ Jack Youngblood

American Football Player

"A strategic victory is seen as luck by laymen."

— Toba Beta, My Ancestor, Was an Ancient Astronaut

"Sure, there are little victories here and there that may seem like lucky breaks, but luck is simply when preparation meets opportunity."

— Ari Herstand

"The phrase "It's better to be lucky than good." must be one of the most ridiculous homilies ever uttered. In nearly any competitive endeavor, you have to be damned good before luck can be of any use to you at all."Garry Kasparov, Deep Thinking: Where Machine Intelligence Ends and Human Creativity Begins

"Luck is believing you are lucky."

— Tennessee Williams

"If there is no door open for me, I build a door."

— Hadi Farnoud

"Luck often sides with the able."

— R.A. Delmonico

"Don't wait for things to happen by luck because it is an uncertain thing anyway."

— Giridhar Alwar, My Quest For Happy Life

"Luck is when those who are prepared take advantage of the moment."

— Raymond E. Feist, Rise of a Merchant Prince

"Meticulousness is the better part of serendipity."

— Reginald Hill, Ruling Passion

"Luck is made by making the right choices at the right timing and place."

— Steven Redhead, Life Is Simply A Game

"When I am ready for the opportunity, I get lucky."

`~ Debasish Mridha, M.D.*

Physician, Philosopher, and Author

Back To Scouting References

Please forgive the following repetition. The first rank in Scouting is the *Scout* rank. The badge for the Scout rank consists of a simple fleur-de-lis, which symbolizes a compass needle. The needle points the Scout in the correct direction, onward and upward. From the first rank, scouting is teaching a path to follow and methods for managing one's life and success.

Ranks of Scouting

- Scout
- Tenderfoot
- Second Class
- First Class
- Star
- Life
- Eagle

These ranks are all about acquiring skills. *Eagle* is the highest rank earned in Scouting.

The Eagle rank requires even more skill, but the principal distinction is demonstrating community service and leadership. The Eagle rank requires vital leadership positions in the troop's organization and conceiving, managing, and executing significant community service projects.

Demonstrated leadership is the crucial element distinguishing the Eagle rank as the highest in Scouting.

Leadership:

Required Leadership of your own life:

- You must be the leader of yourself
- Your life
- Your Career
- Your Family
- Your Community
- Your Future

Foresight

A key element of leadership (of luck) is the ability to predict probable outcomes and whether a course of action will lead to a positive or negative result. Through training and discipline, a leader makes good plans, decisions, and choices that will lead to better outcomes.

An experienced leader will develop foresight.

A good leader can predict success and failure by analyzing

the behavior patterns of others.

Good leaders actively avoid trouble and seek opportunities.

Good leaders appear to be lucky.

Good leaders make their luck with careful planning, hard work, and foresight.

Good leadership is especially vital in times of disaster or significant hardship. Sometimes, we have bad luck, even when we have done everything right. But the difference for lucky people is that they have prepared themselves to handle unexpected trouble. *Lucky* people will deal with and turn around even the biggest problems.

Types of Preparation:

- Stocked supplies
- Emergency Management Training
- Advanced First Aid Training
- Self-defense training
- Physical fitness
- Contingency preplanning
- Emergency funds
- Practical skills
- Leadership experience
- A solid network of functional friends
- Personal emotional stability

Preparation is what sets lucky people apart. Even if a

meteorite lands squarely on the lucky person's head, if he lives, he will deal with the problem and get on with his life with whatever he is left with. Lucky people are unstoppable. (They will also, later, tell a great story about it.)

Elements of Good Luck

- Forethought
- Thoughtful planning
- Developed foresight
- Safety consciousness
- Preparation
    - Education
    - Training
    - Experience
    - Positioning
    - Savings
- Consistent hard work
- Ethics
- Professional and social networking
- Good people choosing (judicious associations)
- Skills development
- Accumulated tools
- Perseverance
- Leadership
- Community service

Examples of Physical Preparation:

- Fire extinguishers
- First aid kit
- Emergency funds
- Emergency supplies
- Self-defense strategies
- Training
- Weapons
- Established protocols

What You Know

An old saying is, "It's not what you know; it's who you know."

There may be some truth to that, but the *who* will offer you little in return if you have little to provide that influential person. The truth is, it is both *what* you know and *who* you know.

Leaders tend to network with other leaders. If you have something important to offer, you will probably find the people who need you if you are socially and professionally active and busy.

The next chapter is all about *who you know*. Or, more to the point, who you *choose* to know.

"The best way to improve your luck is to improve your people."

~Bert Wolfe

Conclusion: You make your own luck.

Chapter 18 Head Trips

Who is in Your Head?

Seriously, who is in your head?

Whose goal is that?

Whose idea is that?

Whose value is that?

Whose taste is that?

Whose lifestyle is that?

Who said you needed to live there?

Who said you had to go to college?

Who said you should get married?

Who said you should have kids?

Who told you that?

Do they know what they are talking about?

Do they have self-serving ulterior motives?

Is their advice based in fear?

Are they attempting to make themselves right for the decisions they believed they should have made?

Should you follow their advice?

Do they have the results you want?

Do you agree with their advice?

Are they offering insight into their wisdom or are they impinging their pedantic opinion on you?

There is an old saying that opinions are like assholes; everyone has one. I disagree; people only have one asshole, but they have lots of opinions about almost everything.

So, expect lots of opinions:

- Unfounded opinions
- Half-baked opinions
- Popular opinions
- Repeated opinions
- Informed opinions

All these opinions have in common that they belong to other people and not necessarily to you.

- What is your opinion?
- What is your opinion based on?
- Are you sure that is your opinion?
- Bullshit opinions can be contagious.
- Opinions are passed down through generations.
- Opinions are like onions; they have many layers.

Opinions and advice can be laced with truth but be fundamentally false or misleading.

An excellent way to tell a lie is to frame it with plausible facts, ideas, and opinions.

Don't should on me!

Have you ever had anyone *should* all over you?

- You should this
- You should that
- You should the other thing

Don't let people should on you.

Fear Trips

Ever have someone lay a fear trip on you?

OMG:

- "If you do that."
- If you don't do this."
- "You should have done this."
- "You should not have done that."
- "You know what is going to happen."
- "Better be careful."

Acromyms for the word, fear:

- False evidence appears real
- False emotions appear real
- False expectations about reality
- False events appearing real
- Foreseen events appearing real
- False expectations about reality
- False entity appearing real
- Forgetting everything is alright
- Forgetting everything about reality
- Forget everything and run
- Feel emotion and run
- Frantic efforts to avoid reality
- Finding excuses and reasons
- Failure expected and received

Conclusion: Be of one mind – yours!

Chapter 19 Choose Your People

Choose Your People

With whom do you choose to associate?

"It's not what we have in life, but who we have in our life that matters."

~Unknown

"The best way to improve your luck is to choose your people carefully."

~Bert Wolfe

"If you find that you are the smartest person in the room, you need a new room."

~Unknown

"I have made it my business to associate with smarter, richer, and more powerful people than I am. My challenge has been to find things to offer these people in exchange for their continued company without degrading my self-worth while continuing to improve myself."

~Bert Wolfe

"You can't soar with eagles while down on the ground
with turkeys."

~Unknown

Of Whom Do I Need to Divest?

Over the years, I have divested myself of people who don't strive for improvement.

I have phased out friends with too little to contribute to conversations and projects.

My associates need to be some combination of:

- Funny
- Ethical
- Deep thinking
- Inspiring
- Enterprising
- Adventurous
- Entertaining
- Generous

I endeavor to reciprocate with my own combination of resources and knowledge to contribute to the conversation.

Purposely hang out with people who are:

- Smarter
- Richer
- More creative
- More honorable
- More fun
- More productive
- More generous
- More ambitious
- More visionary
- More altruistic

Toxic People

Various authors have identified toxic personalities that are very much to be avoided. Don't spar with toxic people. Don't compete with them. Don't try to correct them. Don't try to help them. I am not kidding; phase these people out of your life. Don't accept their invitations. Don't invite them to events. Phase them out of your life. Your good luck depends on it.

Toxic Personality Traits:

- Toxic Arrogance
- Toxic Victimhood
- Toxic Controller
- Toxic Envy
- Toxic Lier
- Toxic Negativity
- Toxic Critic
- Toxic Greed
- Toxic Judgmentalism
- Toxic Gossip
- Toxic Lack of Character
- Toxic Neglect

Another List of Toxic Types:

- The gossip
- The temperamental
- The victim
- The complainer
- The self-absorbed
- The envious
- The manipulator

- The dementor
- The twisted
- The judgmental
- The arrogant

Another List:

- The narcissist
- The chronic downer
- The critic
- The contrarian
- The underminer
- The flake
- The betrayer
- The rival
- The big-mouth
- The bad-influence

Unhealthy Signs That They are Psychologically Toxic:

- They are controlling
- They are jealous
- They lie
- They play victim
- They gossip

- They are greedy
- They neglect
- They always come first
- They are contrary
- They are disagreeable
- They are negative
- They are arrogant
- They are always right
- They are critical
- They are competitive
- They are nosey
- They are needy
- They are demanding
- They are selfish

A **narcissist** is a highly self-centered person with an exaggerated sense of self-importance; a person who has an excessive interest in or admiration for themselves and thinks the world revolves around them. Narcissists can be anywhere around you.

"Love doesn't die a natural death. Love has to be killed by neglect or narcissism."

Lovesagame.com

"You feel on edge around this person, but still, you want them to like you."

www.yourtango.com

"I loved you head over handles

like my first bicycle accident

Before the mouthful of blood and gravel,

I swore we were flying."

~Poet Unknown

A **sociopath** is a person with little to no conscience. They will lie, exploit, cheat, and steal from you. Sociopaths manipulate others for their benefit. They know what they are doing; they don't care about you. They seem friendly and charming at first, almost too nice, but it's fake. The niceness will last until a problem occurs in which they are at fault; however, they will manipulate you into believing that you are the one who is wrong. They will transfer blame, redirect conversations, deflect your inquiries, and move or redefine the target to suit their desired outcome. Shame, blame, and guilt are their favorite tools. Sociopathy is a personality disorder. A sociopath will often exhibit charm and charisma but only care about themselves. Sociopaths avoid punishment, so they tend not to break laws.

A **psychopath** has a chronic mental disorder, often with violent social behavior. They are mentally unstable. A psychopath is a sociopath who is a criminal. A psychopath will readily break laws and commit harm. Typically, they have a selfish and antisocial personality marked by a lack of remorse for their actions and an absence of empathy for others. They lack any ability to love or establish meaningful personal relationships. They have no morals, and they utterly lack empathy and remorse.

The Distinction

My take on the distinction between a sociopath and a psychopath is that a *sociopath* lacks a conscience but avoids social and legal consequences. The sociopath plays it safe by hiding their lack of conscience while keeping their behavior inside social expectations. The sociopath is aware that, unlike himself, you have a conscience, and the sociopath considers this to be a personal weakness on your part. The sociopath will manipulate you by leveraging your conscience, sense of honor, and morality. The sociopath is the grifter, confidence artist, swindler, embezzler, etc.

The *psychopath*, on the other hand, is not inhibited by laws and morality. This is the violent, remorseless criminal, rapist, pedophile, armed robber, carjacker, murderer, etc.

Neither can be trusted. Neither can be rehabilitated. Ward them off; don't associate with them.

Sociopaths will insinuate themselves into otherwise wholesome groups and activities.

The narcissist has a grandiose sense of self-importance, lacks empathy, and needs attention and admiration while exhibiting an exaggerated sense of entitlement.

Narcissism is discussed ad nauseam in popular literature. I don't feel the need to parse out distinctions in defective personalities. Learn to recognize unwholesome people and avoid them.

Carefully choose the people you hang out with.

Psychologically Nutritious People

"If there are so-called toxic people, there must be psychologically nutritious people."

~Bert Wolfe

Unhealthy Signs that a Person is Psychologically Toxic:	Healthy Counterparts: Signs of Healthy Associations:
They are controlling	They control themselves, not others
They are jealous	They admire the success of others
They chronically compare themselves to others	They observe and learn from others
They lie	They tell their own truth
They play victim	They take responsibility for their conditions
They gossip	They speak well of others
They are greedy	They are generous
They always come first	They can put others' needs before their own
They are negative	They have a positive attitude
They are critical	They are supportive

They are competitive	They are collaborative
They are arrogant	They are confidently humble
They are always right	Able to see their own mistakes
They are nosey	They respect privacy
They lack boundaries	Sensitive to other's boundaries
They are needy	They take care of themselves (and others)
They are selfish	They are giving, helpful, and caring

This chart is too black and white, but it gives you an idea of what to watch for. Everybody has some careless, toxic behavior, so don't throw the baby out with the bathwater.

Become self-aware; which characteristics on the list apply to you?

Carefully choose the people with whom you associate.

"Be careful what you tolerate. You are teaching people how to treat you.

~Unknown

"Before you diagnose yourself with depression or low self-esteem, first make sure you are not, in fact, just surrounded by assholes."

~Unknown

Recommended books:

Emotional Intelligence 2.0

By Travis Bradberry

The Sociopath Next Door

By Martha Stout

"People inspire you, or they drain you—pick them wisely."

~ Hans F. Hansen

Retired Football Player

"Great minds discuss ideas; average ones discuss events,
and small minds discuss people."

~ Eleanor Roosevelt

Former First Lady of The United States

FLOTUS

So, who do we choose?

Look for people who are:

- Ethical
- Smart
- Loving
- Contributing
- Collaborative
- Accommodating
- Intellectual
- Energetic
- Enterprising
- Adventurous
- Well-traveled
- Community leader
- Trustworthy
- Appreciative
- Loyal
- Cheerful

- Kind-hearted
- Generous
- Socially graceful
- Altruistic
- Forgiving
- Confident, but
- Humble

"Take good care of the people who take good care of you."

~Bert Wolfe

Conclusion: Methodically choose your people. The people you choose will determine the outcomes of your life.

Chapter 20 Gumption

What is Gumption?

Gumption

Shrewd or spirited initiative and resourcefulness; courage, guts, energy of mind and body, enthusiasm, boldness of enterprise, industry, grit, nerve, spunk, drive; the ability to decide what is the best thing to do in a particular situation, and to do it with energy and determination; fortitude and determination.

Where does gumption come from? Are we born with gumption?

Most people who exhibit gumption were born with it, and gumption seems to be part of their nature.

On the other hand, I have observed chronically lazy dullards suddenly discovering a keen interest in something or developing a passion for some activity or endeavor, and they just light up and take off.

Sometimes, gumption is triggered by some outside threat or some imminent danger of loss of some kind. Sometimes, gumption suddenly becomes triggered when someone they love is threatened, and the situation demands robust and decisive action.

For gumption to be useful financially, you must sustain it indefinitely.

A short burst of gumption might solve an emergency, but long-term gumption is required to build anything substantial. Even mild gumption applied consistently over time can achieve great things.

Other words for gumption:

- Enterprising
- Motivated
- Determined
- Ernest
- Ardent
- Initiative
- Boogie power
- Dedication
- Moxie
- Unstoppable intention
- Drive
- Work ethic
- True grit
- Enterprise
- Ingenuity
- Shrewdness

- Resourcefulness
- Inventiveness
- Enterprise
- Industry
- Ambition
- Initiative
- Enthusiasm
- Get-up-and-go
- Vigor
- Aspiration
- Ambition
- Zeal
- Passion

Some people appear to have no gumption. How can a person show no initiative? Is laziness a psychological condition? Are some people born lazy? Lack of gumption could be considered a serious disability.

Some People are Obtuse

To be obtuse is not just to be dim; it suggests a refusal to see something apparent to others or willful ignorance or insensitivity to the facts of a situation. An obtuse person is annoyingly insensitive or slow to understand, and they lack sharpness or quickness of sensibility or intellect: "He is too obtuse to take a hint."

"If you don't burn out at the end of each day, you're a bum."

~ George Lois

"Talent is what God gives us; Skill is what we give back to Him."

~ Eliel Pierre

"The only thing that overcomes hard luck is hard work."

~ Harry Golden

What is talent?

Natural aptitude or skill:

- flair
- aptitude
- facility
- gift
- knack
- technique
- touch
- bent
- ability
- skill
- adeptness

- prowess
- mastery
- artistry
- natural ability

Talent is an exceptional natural ability, especially in a particular activity, such as music, a kind of ability that comes without training - something you're born with. It is contrasted with skill, an ability acquired and developed through practice.

Where does talent come from?
- Inborn?
- Developed?

What is Skill?

Where does skill come from?
- Learning?
- Training?
- Practicing?
- Drilling?
- Rehearsing?

What is the distinction between talent and skill?

We can develop skills; can we develop talent?

Where does 'drive' come from?

Some people seem naturally energetic but unfocused, the classic chicken running around with his head cut off. It seems like drive might be energy-focused on a need, want, or goal of some importance.

Most people I have known exhibit some kind of talent; the trick is to discover the talent and make good use of it.

https://youtu.be/AynXoLjYrKc

Aptitude: the natural ability to do something:

Synonyms:

- talent
- skill
- expertise
- expertness
- adeptness
- skillfulness
- prowess
- mastery
- artistry
- accomplishment
- competence
- proficiency

- dexterity
- adroitness
- deftness
- enthusiasm
- cleverness
- smartness
- knack
- brilliance
- genius

Aptitude might be considered an ingredient for demonstrating competence, while competence, given some drive, could lead to good performance.

We are not looking for potential; we need effective performance.

Components of competence:

- Aptitude
- Talent
- Intelligence
- Knowledge
- Education
- Experience

- Training
- Drilling
- Rehearsing

Ingredients of Consistent, Useful Performance:

- Competence (aptitude, IQ, talent, skill)
- Knowledge (education, training, experience)
- Gumption (need, willpower, drive)
- Boogie Power (strong initiative)

Aptitude is a component of competence at a particular level of quality. Outstanding aptitude is considered 'talent.' An aptitude may be physical or mental. Aptitude is the inborn potential to do certain kinds of work, whether developed or undeveloped. Ability is developed knowledge, understanding, learned or acquired abilities (skills), or attitude. The innate nature of aptitude contrasts skills and achievement, representing knowledge or ability gained through learning.

If talent and aptitude are natural gifts, can insipient gifts be elicited and developed to a practical level of proficiency? What could motivate an individual?

Drive might be produced by an essential need to survive on some level.

Needs types:

- Fear
- Guilt
- Avoidance
- Excitement
- Reward
- Possibility
- Fun
- Exhilaration

Types of driving needs:

o To avoid:
  - o Great loss
  - o Embarrassment
  - o Shame
  - o Penalty
  - o Punishment
  - o Pain
o Possibility of great;
  - o Reward
  - o Payoff
  - o Relief
  - o Release
  - o Pleasure
  - o Satisfaction
  - o Accomplishment

- You need to prove yourself to someone
- You need to demonstrate your value to a person or group
- You need to prove someone wrong
- You need to prove yourself right
- You need to pull something off
- The need to do something:
  - Noteworthy
  - Exceptional
  - Cool
- The need to do something no one else has done
- The need to do something beautiful
  - Fun
  - Exciting
  - Memorable
- The need to create:
  - Beauty
  - A legacy
  - History
  - Harmony
  - Trouble

Why Do You Get Up in the Morning?

Earl Nightingale Quotations:

"Success is the progressive realization of a worthy goal or ideal."

"People with goals succeed because they know where they're going."

"The mind moves in the direction of our currently dominant thoughts."

"We can let circumstances rule us, or we can take charge and rule our lives from within."

"Creativity is a natural extension of our enthusiasm."

"Everything begins with an idea."

"What's going on in the inside shows on the outside."

"We tend to live up to our expectations."

"When you judge others, you do not define them; you define yourself."

"Whatever we plant in our subconscious mind and nourish with repetition and emotion will one day become reality."

"You are now, and you do become what you think about."

"Our attitude toward life determines life's attitude towards us."

"Every one of us is the sum total of his own thoughts."

"We become what we think about."

"If you work harder, longer, and smarter than your peers, they won't be your peers for long."

~**Bert Wolfe**

Consistent Effort

What if we consistently worked a little longer and a little smarter every day? What if we added 10% more effort to each day; would it add up to much? Twenty-four times 60 minutes equals 1,440 minutes in a day. Let's subtract sleeping, personal care and feeding, and a job at twenty hours. Let's allot 4 hours a day to personal production. Now let's add 10% effort to those four hours. Four hours is 240 minutes. 10% of 240 minutes is 25 minutes per day, and 365 days in a year equals 9,130 minutes. 9,130 divided by 60 minutes equals 150 hours. That is four weeks of full-time work. Four weeks is a month. So, what if you put in a month's more work than the other guy? Do you think you would get ahead? In ten years, you will have worked a whole year more than the other guy.

In addition to putting in more time than the other guy, what if you also worked smarter than the other guy? If you work harder, longer, and smarter than your peers, they won't be your peers for long.

"Work your ass off."

"Work works."

~Arnold Schwarzenegger

"We are judged by our

Beliefs (our talk),

Actions (our walk), and

Deeds (our accomplishments).

Walk your talk and achieve remarkable things."

~Bert Wolfe

Conclusion: Find your gumption.

Chapter 21 Your Attitude and Disposition

"If you dislike someone, dislike them alone; don't recruit others to join your cause."

~Toby Mac

#SPEAKLIFE

"The pessimist complains about the wind.

The optimist expects it to change.

The leader adjusts the sails."

~ John Maxwell

Maintain Mental Discipline:

- Don't complain
- Maintain a positive mental attitude
- Control your thoughts
- Control the words that come out of your mouth
- Control what you allow others to say to you
- Control how others treat you
- Take good care of your chosen people

- Select and choose the positive members of your family
- Watch your attitude
- Practice good manners
- Be polite
- Control the content of your input
- Carefully choose your people

"Pain is inevitable, but suffering is optional."

~Old saying

There is an interesting distinction between pain and suffering. A Zen master will experience pain without attributing significance to the pain. He will not feel sad or mad. He will not leverage pain to excuse his performance. He will not leverage pain to engender sympathy. He will not own pain; he will not refer to it as his pain; it is the pain, not his pain. Do not allow pain to transmogrify into personal suffering.

~Bert Wolfe

"Honest to God, I can't get anything through my son's thick skull.

I talk to him until I'm blue in the face.

Not for love or money can I get this kid to wake up."

~Overheard by B. W.

"Stop whining, whimpering, and sucking your thumb."

~Bert Wolfe

What if you were born into serious:

- Poverty?
- Illness?
- Disfigured ugliness?
- Stupidity?
- Mental illness?
- Disability?
- Violence?
- Abuse?
- Illiteracy?
- Religious repression?
- Environmental hazards?
- Government repression?

- Social unrest – war?
- Slavery?
- Degradation?

These are ingredients for sad stories. Generally, you can't fix much of this stuff, but you must try not to be handicapped by it.

You probably weren't born into much or any of that, so don't let me catch you sucking your thumb and telling people sad stories about why you aren't winning.

Personal Deficiencies and Disabilities You Can Fix

These are your responsibility – they are not bad luck per se:

- Poor grammar
- Negative attitudes
- Poor posture
- Poor body language
- Weak vocabulary
- Poor education
- Poor health habits
- Poor body image
- Poor self-esteem

"We can't expect to be lucky and prosperous without dealing with our poor qualities. Do an honest inventory and get to work—no excuses for bad manners and grammar."

~Bert Wolfe

"You know, if you're an American and you're born at this time in history especially, you're lucky. We all are. We won the world history Powerball lottery."

~ Bill Maher

Nowadays, there is no excuse for complaining and not getting on with a fantastic life. If nothing on the above list applies to you, then you have it made. So, don't blow your incredible advantages by making thoughtless decisions and mistakes about marriage, children, and careers.

Conclusion: Have an attitude of gratitude.

Chapter 22 Learn to Say No

"No may be the most important word in your spoken

vocabulary."

~Bert Wolfe

The *No* Exercise

No may be the most powerful word in your vocabulary.

Most of us have a tough time saying *no*. We often feel uncomfortable saying no – even when we know we must say no.

Most of us have been trained and conditioned by our parents, schools, and churches to be helpful, cooperative, and generous. We have been brainwashed to say *yes*. That's nice for everybody we say yes to, but when and where do we say no?

You always have the right to turn down an invitation or refuse a requested favor, and it's okay to prioritize your needs. Sometimes, to be agreeable, we slip toward the point of being *compliant*. If you don't learn to say no, your life energy will be consumed by other people being served by you.

If you can't say no, you will be exploited.

The following is a life-changing exercise:

When no one else is home, lock yourself in your bathroom and look at yourself in the mirror. Stare yourself right in the eyes and say <u>no</u>. Say <u>no</u> to yourself. Say <u>no</u> to yourself repeatedly.

Practice saying no to yourself using every kind of emotion and inflection you can think of:

- No, thank you.
- Um, no.
- Hmm, no.
- Wow. No.
- No harm in asking, but no.
- I need to say no to that.
- I'm afraid that is a firm *no*.
- I'm flattered that you would ask me, but no.
- Are you kidding? No.
- You can't be serious. No.
- Seriously? Nice try. No.
- That is a solid, definite no.
- That's a hard no.
- Never in your dreams. No.

- Hell no!

- Not now, not ever, no.

- No.

Children, especially, need to be taught to say no. Learning to say no is an integral part of safety training for kids, and we all need to establish personal boundaries. Teach your children how to say no. And teach them how to mean it when they say no. Teach children how to convey their convictions to others.

Reasons you say yes when you should say no:

- You are *nice*[12].

- You are a people pleaser.

- You avoid conflict.

- You are prone to guilt.

- You are uncomfortable with confrontation.

- You want to be liked.

- You feel obliged.

- You have low self-worth.

- You feel that you owe something.

---

[12] "No more Mister Nice Guy" because "Nice guys finish last."

- You think you need to *give back*[13].

Part of learning to say no is learning to not say yes. Learn not to say yes automatically. The counterpart to learning to say no is to know when and when not to say yes. We are conditioned to say yes to requests automatically, so we must be highly conscious of our responses to questions and requests. We need to learn that saying yes can lead to non-optimum situations. We are taught to be cooperative and compliant. From now on, go to *high alert* when someone makes a request.

Learn to say no without feeling guilty; Setting boundaries is healthy. You need to respect and take care of yourself. Learn the art of saying no. Don't lie. Don't make excuses, and don't over-explain yourself; Just decline.

It is simple to say no when your priorities are clear.

---

[13] What is *giving back*? I don't understand this expression. Do people think they took too much at some point? Who did they take it from?

Friends can be persuasive. They may sincerely want you to participate, and they may ask more than once, hoping you will change your mind. For their part, there is no real harm in this. The harm comes when you say yes when you know you should say no.

Life is short. Use your time wisely. Say no if the activity is not fun, wholesome, and on track with your personal goals.

It's okay to say *no*.

It's your life. Take charge of it.

"It's only by saying NO that you can concentrate on the things that are really important."

~ Steve Jobs

"You have to decide what your highest priorities are and have the courage to pleasantly, smilingly, and non-apologetically say no to other things. And the way to do that is by having a bigger yes burning inside."

~ Stephen Covey

Conclusion: Learn to say no.

Chapter 23 Is It Too Late?

Have you already made too many mistakes? Is it too late?

I don't know.

It is probably too late for the *common man* who follows *conventional wisdom*. However, recovery stories are plentiful, and it seems that an effective attitude, determination, and hard work can overcome significant losses and obstacles.

"We all have big changes in our lives that are more or less a second chance."

~Harrison Ford

"It's amazing how a little tomorrow can make up for a whole lot of yesterday."

~John Guare

Playwright

"I can't change the direction of the wind, but I can adjust my sails to always reach my destination."

~Jimmy Dean

Country Music Singer

"After twenty years on a Mountain Rescue team, I concluded that it's rarely too late to improve a bad situation. Rescuers meet people on one of the worst days of their lives. If the subject doesn't die, they get another chance to live. I always hope they make the best of their second chance."

~Bert Wolfe

"You can't go back and change the beginning, but you can start where you are and change the ending."

~C. S. Lewis

Financial recovery will be daunting for a person who already has children from one or two failed marriages. Rebuilding a life is not easy, but it can be done.

Changes and strict policies must be put into place:

- Get pregnancy proof.
- Do not remarry.
- Focus on your income like a demon.
- Do not commute.
- Lower your expenses with a passion.
- Live like an ascetic monk.
- Do not pay for your children's higher education.
- Do not support offspring over the age of 18.
- Get regular personal counseling.
- Exercise rigorously.
- Have compelling outside interests.
- Get a lot of sleep.
- Create passive income.
- Find ways to have fun.
- <u>Keep your life balanced.</u>

Lead a balanced lifestyle. Do not neglect yourself. Take care of yourself so you are better able to serve your family. Build a lifestyle based on moderation, variety, and consistency.

Divorces happen because *things* are out of balance; the marital partners are chronically dissatisfied and frustrated. Divorce is a complex and emotionally fraught process with significant consequences for those involved. Divorce will profoundly impact the lives of the divorcing couple, their children, and their wider social circle. You must keep your life balanced if you want to rebuild.

Conclusion: Do not let yourself backslide into the frame of mind that led you to financial disaster.

Chapter 24 Review and Conclusion

"If common sense were common, most people would have it. The truth is that few people have <u>good judgment</u>, and good judgment is what we're looking for to make a good life."

~Bert Wolfe

I posit that when people do stupid things, some combination of these things is in play:

- They have a low IQ.
- They have low self-esteem.
- They have a mental illness.
- They have crippling fear.
- They have learning disabilities that they have failed to overcome.
- They are poorly educated (ignorant) (and lacking critical information.)
- They lack the focus, habits, training, and discipline to analyze situations.
- They let emotions override logic.
- They have been cripplingly indoctrinated (brainwashed) into false ideas and beliefs.
- They are actively associating with a toxic person.

Intelligence and Wisdom

- **Intelligence** is the capacity to acquire knowledge, skills, and understanding.

- An **Intelligence Quotient** is a number used to express apparent relative intelligence, such as a score determined by a person's performance on a standardized intelligence test compared to the average performance of others of the same age. IQ is akin to computer processing speed.

- An **Intelligent** person can think, learn, and understand new situations without using predetermined, scripted, or thoughtless habits.

- An **automaton** is a person who operates on habitual, routine mental circuits rather than freshly analyzing circumstances as they come up.

- **Wisdom** is the judicious use of experience and knowledge.

- A **wise** person can interpret given circumstances, experience, and knowledge to make sound judgments and decisions.

Even when we are too young or new to a subject to have acquired true wisdom, we can apply our intelligence to seek wisdom from wise people. We can use other people's discernment to help make good decisions and choices.

Take Time to Think

Most people are careening through life with no particular plan and simply defaulting their decision-making to genetic programming and social indoctrination. Most people operate as if they are fundamentally unconscious or hypnotized. Most people have never really evaluated their own intelligence and personal savvy.

There seem to be many types of human intelligence.

Types of smart:

- intellectual
- street smart
- savvy
- clever
- sharp
- sensible
- bright
- brainy
- etc.

So, what kind of smart are you?

There are all kinds of intelligence and wisdom. Consider the various distinctions:

- Intelligence
- Wisdom
- Common knowledge

- *Conventional wisdom*
- *Common sense*
- Good sense
- Good judgement
- Practical thinking
- Emotional intelligence
- Financial Intelligence
- Social Intelligence
- "Book smart and life stupid."
- "Bus smart and school stupid."
- "Office smart and street stupid."
- "Job smart and family stupid."
- "Home smart and public stupid."

"Intelligence and education are often confused as words and concepts. Not-so-smart people can have lots of education, whereas a genius can sorely lack education."

~Bert Wolfe

For the most part, we are stuck with the IQ we were born with. We can perhaps leverage our given IQ with disciplined hard work, lots of sleep, and brain exercises, but we are stuck with what we have for all practical purposes. So, make the best of it.

The saving grace and secret weapon for all of us with average IQs is *education* - and lots of it. I mean *formal education*, but I especially mean *self-education*.

The other secret weapon is to take the time to truly think. Use the brainpower you have to consider your options before making significant decisions. And have a plan and personal policies on which to base your choices.

Sometimes, someone will say, "What were they thinking?!" My typical reply is, "I don't think they were."

Don't hurry into decisions. Take the time to think. Look before you leap. There can be significant differences between mere urgencies and actual emergencies. Most of life's big decisions are not emergencies, and we are rarely required to make immediate decisions about the significant actions of our lives. But procrastination is the enemy during an urgency. So, consider everything you can and make that decision so you can move forward.

Occasionally, I get accused of procrastinating by someone who knows I am delaying a big decision or project. However, my history has shown that I don't really procrastinate. During the apparent delay, I am considering and contemplating. I am planning, designing, and choosing. I am waiting for the correct timing. I make sure my projects and decisions align with my life goals and personal policies.

I want the timing to be strategically harmonious for everyone involved.

The truth is that once I reach a point of personal resolve, the world had better get out of my way. After I finish "procrastinating," I am like a fast-moving freight train.

Once you make your plan, stick to it. You can fine-tune your life plan as you move through time, but do not jump around making whole new plans once you are underway.

If you analyze the failure patterns of a frustrated loser, you will consistently discover that:

- The person does not have a clear, well-developed life plan.
- The person pursued a series of half-baked inspirations.
- The person does not have detailed personal policies.
- The person has no clear guiding philosophy of life.
- The person makes significant decisions with little forethought.
- The person's energy and initiative are inconsistent.
- The person is associated with toxic people.
- The person has a carelessly risky lifestyle.
- The person wastes a lot of time.
- The person does not live by a code of ethics.
- The person does not live by a code of honor.

Overview of successful actions that lead to successful outcomes:

- Make your life plan.
- Develop your personal policies.
- Follow your plans and policies.
- Think before you marry.
- "Marry before you carry."
- Think before you procreate.
- Get a strategic education.
- Develop a career that supports your goals.
- Live in a safe and prosperous place.
- Live close to where you work.
- Avoid significant life changes:
  - Houses
  - Spouses
  - Careers
- Understand the stages of life.
- Optimize your time.
- Be fiscally intelligent.
- Enjoy a fun, safe, modest lifestyle.
- Foster good luck.
- Live by a code of honor.
- Selectively choose your people.
- Continually review and assess your life.

Make a deep, personal inquiry before you make any significant life decisions.

Earnestly ask yourself these questions:

- Why that particular mate?
- Why get married?
- Why have children?
- Why that education?
- Why that career?
- Why live in that community?
- Why that dwelling?
- Why that commute?
- Why that lifestyle?
- Why these people?
- Why that sport?

Please don't engage in any of these activities without answering your questions.

The purpose of this book is to encourage people to make deep personal inquiries into their most important life decisions with the target of better outcomes.

Play the Hand You are Dealt

Some people seem to have been born with significant advantages:

- Good looking
- Healthy body
- Family money
- Family position
- High IQ
- Private schooling
- Culture, class, and social position
- Family network of influential contacts
- Born in a prosperous city, state, or country
- Lucky genetics

Good for them; I hope they don't waste these advantages.

The family you were born into might look more like this:

- Poor
- Ignorant
- Third world
- Chronic disruption
- Terrible diet
- Poor grammar
- Lack of manners
- Poor health
- Unattractive

Okay, sad for you. You can tell your sad story once, per acquaintance, only once. Repeatedly telling a sad story to explain your lack of success is a coward's path.

Occasionally, someone will tell me their sad story to brag about how far they have progressed. Fair enough, but avoid being boorish or braggadocios about it.

Be prudent about telling your sad stories. It can create sadness and unneeded empathy from your friends, lowering your perceived status.

Learn to be gracious and effective despite all disadvantages, setbacks, and failures. Tell your sad stories only on a limited basis. Maybe, if you are coaching someone for success, you tell personal hardship stories to gain rapport and authenticity.

The point is, never degrade yourself by trying to explain away your shortcomings by telling a sad story.

Glass Ceilings (socio/economic prejudice)

- Poor grammar
- Unfortunate regional accents
- Poor table manners
- Poor grooming and hygiene
- Wardrobing ignorance
- Social shyness
- Self-deprecation
- Failure to self-promote

- Failure to use positioning
- Failure to self-educate
- Off-putting personality traits

There are no excuses for these social handicaps. Work on them, and fix them. Just do it.

If you identify with your poor grammar or an unfortunate accent as *who you are*, get over it and eliminate it. Don't worry about friends and family who may tell you not to "get above your raising." They will get over it, or not; who cares? Don't let other people hold you down. Get educated, get trained, get lucky, move up, and win.

Negative Emotions that need to be managed:

- Fear
- Guilt
- Needing to escape
- Envy
- Competitive urges
- Jealousy
- Resentment

You Make Your Own Luck

Sometimes, someone says, *"I have been unlucky in love."*

And I think, *"What? You make your own luck."*

Effectively, they are saying, "I have made poor choices and messed up my relationships."

Sometimes, I hear people denigrating and disparaging their former mates. And I think, *"What?! You are the one who chose them for yourself."*

For people who have made themselves lucky, opportunities are endlessly abundant.

Preparing for opportunities is the trick; being prepared takes forethought and work, and being well prepared is never a happenstance.

> ***"Luck is what happens when preparation meets opportunity."***
>
> *~Seneca*

> *The Boy Scout motto:*
>
> *"Be Prepared"*

Conclusion:

Prepare yourself for good luck.

I want you to be lucky.

Get out there and be lucky.

Make yourself an extraordinary life.

"I hope I find this book early in my next lifetime."

~Bert Wolfe

About the Author

Bert Wolfe has a 30-year background in pastoral counseling. Ordained in two religious traditions, he holds an honorary Doctor of Divinity degree. In addition to his business background, Bert is an author and landlord. He is an avid outdoorsman and world adventurer.

Made in the USA
Columbia, SC
18 April 2025

56812866R10204